Ms. Jessup:

Hope your staff gives you this book. Hope you read it. Hope you like it. And if you do, hope you will recommend it to your friends and promote it the best you can. Thanks.

IsoloMetrik Society

Nikhil Modi

To the human race

Table of Contents

Prologue:

In IsoloMetrik Society, all its citizens should be able to live in peace and dignity and prosper to the best of their abilities unless they are corrupt, criminals or unpatriotic.

IMS is a Society of laws, a Society governed by a rule book.

Article 1

Society and Democracy

IsoloMetrik Society is a democratic society.

A republic to be precise. Ordinary citizens elect representatives who they think will represent their best interests. These representatives will be well compensated and it will be their duty to study all issues that affect their constituents and vote accordingly. Most of the issues should not be left for individual constituent to decide as ordinary citizens neither have the time nor the inclination to study and research every little issue that needs to be voted on. That is why citizens elect presidents, prime ministers, governors, chief ministers as well as state or provincial council members. These are the people who develop expertise on every issue and judge them on behalf of people. The idea of citizens voting on workday government matters may have certain populist appeal but this kind of referendum system soon turns dysfunctional. They rarely reflect accurate public opinion. These single-issue elections are very, very expensive and usually low turnout affairs, so their outcomes depend on which side has more energized base of voters. They are more likely to agitate opponents rather than attract supporters. Throwing too many things on the ballot is never a good idea. It becomes an exercise in extreme democracy which results in chaos. Besides, it usurps the power of locally elected representatives.

Of course, this democracy is an open democracy. In other words, there is see-through transparency. Because, if it is not see-through, it is not run for the masses; it is run on the backs of the masses. Its citizens have the right to freedom of speech, freedom of religion, freedom of assembly, freedom of peaceful protest against government policies, right to join organizations of their choosing that are independent of government, to participate freely in public life and right to equal protection before the law.

In IsoloMetrik Society, rulers (that is the government) are subservient and the ruled (that is the citizens) are superiors. Consent of the masses is the hallmark of the Society. Though it is somewhat inefficient and inconvenient, it is still the best way.

Each country, of course, has the right to choose what kind of democracy would be best suited for its people. But between parliamentary government (Prime Ministerial) and Presidential type of government, IsoloMetrik Society prefers the latter.

In parliamentary style of government, if a political party does not win an absolute majority (and most of the time, it does not) in an election, it has to govern by forming a coalition government. This results in strange bed-fellows. It is cumbersome and lumbering. The work for which masses of people elected the government, does not get done in a smooth manner due to opposing viewpoints and differing loyalties to the causes. Besides, minority parties of the coalition can pull their support on a whim and elected government can collapse any time. A new, fresh election would become necessary in the near future. This is extremely costly monetarily as well as for the psyche of the electorate. It does not auger well for most nations.

In Presidential system, as currently practiced, the president is powerful. However, his hands would also be tied somewhat, if he does not have solid majority in the legislative branches. And the work that he/she was elected to do would be hampered.

IsoloMetrik Society is a democracy with a difference. It restores the balance between democracy and governability. Goal is to carry out welfare of the nation and its people at warp speed. Along with president and Vice President, people will elect a representative (or two, depending on the size and population of a nation) from each of the country's provinces or states. These representatives do have legislative authority but their main function will be to act as a brake against absolute power of a president. The saying *absolute power corrupts absolutely* is very true and IMS cannot let that happen. Unbridled power in the hands of an imperfect (because every human being is imperfect) president can be an unmitigated disaster. So, with a 51% vote, representatives can stop a president from taking certain action deemed detrimental to the country. The president can be impeached or recalled, for due causes (bribery, lying under oath) by a 66% vote. It is assumed here that elected representatives are responsible members who will not act in a frivolous manner. Besides, if one is unable to convince 35% of legislators to side with him/her, what good can you do as a leader anyway? Voters in their provinces can do the same with their own elected representatives. Election should be held every 5 years. Anybody winning a second term, cannot run again for a third term, so that fresh blood and perspective can be brought in. The representatives can also put forward measures or projects that might benefit the citizenry. With 51% of votes in the legislative assembly, these projects may be implemented. President can, of course, oppose these measures and veto them. In that case, with 60% of votes, representatives may override his/her veto.

Similar down ballot logic will be applied to states or provinces of a nation. A governor and representatives will be elected with similar functions, duties, obligations and limitations. So, with a 51% vote, representatives can stop a governor from taking certain action deemed detrimental to the province. The governor can be impeached or recalled with a 66% vote. All processes should be pretty much same at the federal as well as provincial level. Elections should be held at the same time and no individual may run for more than two terms.

Governor will act for the benefit of the state or province while president will act for the benefit of the country. Good of the nation will come before the good of a province while good of a province will come before good of an individual.

President should work in harmony with elected representatives. He can and should solicit ideas from the representatives which may benefit the nation and vice versa. Same with provincial heads and their representatives.

Every citizen has a right to vote and be counted. We recommend that a citizen casting a vote should have a minimum of high school diploma. Some will say this disenfranchises many of a nation's citizens. We beg to differ. In our opinion, this creates a more perfect democracy. We do not allow a ten-year-old to vote as a ten-year-old has not yet developed enough understanding about democracy. We apply the same logic to a high school dropout. In fact, this provision will encourage people to get their high school education. We also recommend that minimum age for voting be 21.

Since there are many, many under-developed, over-populated, poor countries in the world with enormous illiteracy rate, each nation can determine its own appropriate age limit and do away with education requirement, though with utmost caution.

Independent observers, even unbiased international observers, may be appointed to make sure that elections are free and fair. These kinds of free and fair elections will guarantee social rights, bring equality and dignity to its citizenry.

Political art of drawing boundaries to protect incumbents is gerrymandering. The whole idea behind this practice is to carve up the political map for partisan advantage. It has corrosive effects on elections because elections are conducted in districts largely drawn by incumbent politicians for their own benefit. In essence, the politicians choose their own voters, rather than the other way around. Gerrymandering can involve *packing* as well as *cracking*. Packing consists of concentrating voters of one party into a limited number of districts to blunt their influence; cracking entails dispersing them into several different districts to dilute their strength. So, the bottom line would be to make sure that some voters simply do not count as much as others, leaving them effectively disenfranchised. It is very unhealthy for any democracy because it is hard to encourage people to go out and vote when they know they have no real chance of making a difference.

Thus, gerrymandering weakens all political parties and the nation as a whole. Therefore, it is illegal and not allowed by IMS.

Constitution reigns supreme in IsoloMetrik Society and no religious decrees of any kind are allowed. It can only be amended by citizens with 66% vote.

Before concluding this chapter, we will be considered remiss if we do not mention that IsoloMetrik Society is extremely aware as well as wary of Caudillos (Fascists or Authoritarian Populists). They are consummate showmen with a shrewd ability to manage emotions of a large audience and using a mixture of lies and half-truths, pin the blame for all the ills on real or imagined enemies. They confront an ossified political establishment, develop a strong bond with their followers and attack their opponents as well as the media with no holds barred; sometimes even encouraging violence. This movement turns into a cult of personality. The politician becomes an almost messianic figure, towering over all institutions. They become an incarnation of peoples' desires. They are so media savvy that they know what kind of headlines they would like to see the next day and work backwards from there.

Usually they are alpha primates, always on the edge of violence. They have casual disregard for truths. They are narcissists and misogynists. They exhibit self-obsession, ignorance, ingrained vindictiveness and grandiosity. They have an insatiable need for applause.

IMS wants to make sure that *caudillos* do not become prime ministers or presidents. It is good to remember that *caudillos* rise only if people feel abandoned and cheated by the establishment system. They become fed up with imbecile political parties, incapable of efficient governance. IsoloMetrik Society has very strong institutions (Legislative Chamber, Independent Judiciary, Free Press, etc.) and a system of checks and balances to thwart authoritarian populists. Even if they win nominations of their parties, parties can deny them nominations. They will then have to run as independents, minimizing their chances of getting elected.

Article 2

Society and Corruption

We consider corruption as number one cause of misery in this world. It is the evil of all evils. It is one of the most wicked sins that has been allowed to permeate most nations. It is all pervasive and omnipresent. It flows through societies' veins as blood flows through mammals' veins. It has distorted all values, all virtues. Corruption has affected every single aspect of our lives. Every day it is growing massively like a malignant cancer. There is no sphere of social, political, economic, religious activity that seems to be free of corruption. The cost of corruption is so high that it decays and incapacitates nations. People in most of the countries understand and have experienced what corruption has done to them. But it is so embedded in all societies that people think it is a way of life and cannot be eliminated. We are sure many books have been written about ills of corruption. We do not see any need to elaborate further.

Suffice it to say that it is imperative to wipe out corruption from all facets of life. Unless that happens, life of ordinary citizens cannot improve.

IsoloMetrik Society believes that the way to do this is to install an all-encompassing monitoring system. That is not to say that every citizen and every institution should be monitored. But anybody with any kind of power who can accept a bribe and affect the outcome of a decision, *may be* monitored. That would include politicians, ministers, officers, corporate heads among others. Any kind of suspicion of corruption can trigger surveillance. Nobody is immune.

If certain segments of Society feel that they are being monitored more often or more closely than others, so be it. It is perfectly legal. It is not considered discriminatory. Nor does IMS consider surveillance as harassment. In many countries, corruption has become a way of life. Naturally, surveilling also will have to be widespread and all-encompassing in those nations, proportionate to the amount of corruption. Needless to say, monitoring system will have to be extremely sophisticated.

Immediately, this raises privacy issue. We understand that. It is not that we do not respect an individual's right to privacy and freedom. We most certainly do. It is just that corruption is such a debilitating disease that if not removed from its roots, it will keep on gnawing at the heart of a nation until that nation is reduced to its empty, lifeless shell. What we are trying to do is strike a perfect balance between privacy and surveillance. The key which may trigger surveillance is a *well-placed suspicion*.

A special school will be established to train educated individuals in the art of surveillance. Only these highly trained and disciplined individuals can be hired for monitoring. Abuse of monitoring system will not be tolerated. The punishment for unauthorized, intentional, egregious leaks should be very severe.

Punishment for corruption is also very severe. But first, we need to make it clear that underpaid people who accept small bribes to eke out a living is *not* corruption. Only when highly paid people in position of power demand bribes to affect the outcome of a decision is considered corruption. Egregious acts of corruption exceeding all bounds of decency, where financial lives of many innocent citizens are affected, where national interests are irreparably damaged, mean mandatory removal from Society (euphemism for death sentence). If removal from Society is not warranted and yet act of corruption is large enough, heavy financial fine should be imposed such that guilty person may become indigent. For small acts of corruption, warning should be issued and that person may be put on probation. Every case is different and should be judged accordingly.

Since anybody in power may be monitored without their knowledge, chances are very small that they will engage in any kind of corruption. And just in case if they do, they will not be able to escape from the clutches of justice.

Article 3

Society and Crime & Punishment

IsoloMetrik Society believes that crime is one of the most prevailing and damaging aspects of any nation. Crime not only hurts people directly by inflicting physical pain but it harms them psychologically by making them feel insecure, angry, upset, afraid and confused. Victims feel powerless and vulnerable. It limits their opportunities to prosper to the best of their abilities and lead a happy life as much as they otherwise can. These psychological scars can linger a lot longer even after physical scars may have healed. Crimes can affect not only a person against whom a crime is committed; it usually affects family, friends and community as a whole.

That is why crime prevention is IMS's one of the top goals.

IsoloMetrik Society is the most compassionate society. In fact, we are nothing if not compassionate. Our cup runneth over with kindness. Our love is so deep that sometimes it is misunderstood or not understood at all. *We are fine with it.* However, all our compassion is geared towards the victims and none towards the perpetrators of crimes.

This makes us the toughest society for criminals.

We understand that there are many, many root causes of crime. Poverty, unemployment, lack of health care, mental illness, alcoholism, single-parent households, lack of education, teenage pregnancies among others. In fact, IMS has plans to alleviate each and every one of these causes which will be addressed in later chapters.

Here, we will address only the aftermath of commission of crime.

Death by god is the only death acceptable to IMS. Any other unnatural death, inflicted by humans, is not very palatable to the Society.

So, any crime that results in death or grievous injury to the victim, would entail a mandatory death sentence for the perpetrators and their enablers. Each country may decide the best way to carry out this punishment.

Brutal rapes fall under the same category as murder. Each instance of date rape and he said - she said rape has to be examined on a case by case basis and judgment rendered accordingly.

Kidnaping anybody for financial gain or even political gain is considered cruel and ruthless act, which would entail ruthless consequences.

IMS does not distinguish between animal cruelty and cruelty perpetrated on humans. We believe those who can be utterly cruel towards animals, will not be kind towards humans. Besides, animals have same feelings as the humans except that they cannot speak human language. So, punishment will be the same depending on brutality exhibited towards animals.

There is no such thing as escaping on a technicality. Nor any such thing as statute of time limitations for prosecuting a crime.

Once a crime is committed, it does not matter if the perpetrators are insane, mentally incompetent, minors or come from a depraved upbringing.

Intent is an important factor in determining punishment. But lack of intent may not be enough to mitigate a crime. If a person goes with the intention of merely scaring or robbing someone and fires a gun which severely wounds or kills the victim, it is still a capital punishment crime. Besides, it is very difficult to prove lack of intent. In IsoloMetrik Society, when a crime is committed, evil intent is presumed.

If someone steals a car and nobody gets hurt, one-time probation may be given. Same consequence for burglarizing a home or business.

If one puts a gun to some body's head to rob a person's purse or wallet, one-time probation may or may not be given, even though, in this instance, trigger was not pulled. Society presumes that trigger would have been pulled had the victim not acquiesced. We are still willing to evaluate each case on its own.

If a person plans to knock-off somebody and hires others to carry out the crime, but the crime is never actually committed for some reason or those *others* turn out to be undercover police officers, that act of planning itself is sufficient to hang the planner as well as all of the enablers, if any.

Gangs deemed harmful to law abiding citizens will not be allowed to exist.

Ordinary citizens of the Society work hard to bring food on the table, educate their children and go about raising a family in their own simple ways. They neither have the time nor the tools to handle lawless marauding gangs who try their best to make life miserable for these decent law-abiding families. The burden falls on elected officials of the government to keep them safe and secure. IsoloMetrik Society is determined not to fail in this effort.

Carrying an unlicensed weapon is a felony and may be cause enough to remove a person from the Society, depending on who is carrying it and the weapon carried. We feel that chances are strong that that weapon in wrong hands will invariably be used to harm another person. Again, each case merits its own treatment. Some civil-liberties activists will howl saying this leads to discrimination against minorities and poor people. At first glance, it may seem that way but in the eyes of IsoloMetrik Society, this is neither discrimination nor harassment. Our intent here is merely to prevent future crimes. We have full faith in judges trained by the Society.

Society has a vast and extremely sophisticated surveilling system and it allows any person, any institution to be monitored. If some members of the Society feel they are being watched more intensely or more often than others, so be it. What is not allowed is random harassment, beating of individuals, molesting of denizens. IMS does not consider surveilling as harassment. On the contrary, Society considers this a prudent policy. In certain high crime areas, stop and frisk is a good thing.

Again, we cannot emphasis strongly enough that Society has no other ulterior motive with our surveillance, except preventing crimes that would hurt law abiding citizens.

There are no prisons in IsoloMetrik Society.

Either there is acquittal, probation, financial liability, corporal punishment and of course, removal from Society when the crime warrants it. So, there will be no need for prisons anywhere in IMS nations. There may be temporary holding cells until guilt or innocence of the accused is proven.

Trial should only be held to prove guilt or innocence of the accused. In obvious cases of guilt, there is no need for any trial. If there is a video or verifiable audio of a person committing a heinous crime and that person can be identified, Society does not believe in wasting anybody's time to conduct a lengthy trial. DNA evidence may also be irrefutable.

In some cases, physical punishment may be appropriate or heavy financial burden may be imposed.

In IsoloMetrik Society, you are innocent until proven guilty.

Society does not believe in jury trial. To select a jury, to sit a jury, to explain the law to laymen is totally unnecessary. It delays the trial and its outcome. Besides, for shrewd lawyers, it is easier to bamboozle a jury consisting of ordinary citizens. Qualified judges are the best people to conduct speedy trials. A panel of three (or five) educated and trained persons is appointed to hear the case and see the evidence. A simple majority is needed for any decision. Each town, city, state or province may have its own panel of judges. A guilty verdict at the local level may be appealed once to the apex court. Decision of the supreme court is final. Society believes most trials should be completed within a week and judgment of guilt or innocence rendered. If found guilty, appropriate punishment should be carried out within approximately three days. Criminals who deserve removal from Society will be cremated regardless of their preferences and their ashes will not be returned to their families.

Speedy trial does not mean shoddy trial. In IMS, all trials are conducted in an impeccable manner.

In fact, we are very proud to say that not a single innocent person would ever be hanged by the Society. Either there is an *honest* proof of guilt or there is not.

Eyewitness testimony of a witness is not enough to determine guilt. Eyes sometimes do deceive. Five or six people ganging up on the accused may also not be enough if they have an axe to grind. Characters of witnesses is very important.

If the Society has gut feelings about the guilt of the accused but not solid proof of guilt, that person should be released simply because IMS does not want gratuitous blood on its hands. However, that person then may be monitored closely. If the person is guilty, sooner or later he/she will trip up and provide necessary proof.

In IsoloMetrik Society, there is no such thing as double jeopardy. It also does not distinguish between juvenile crime and adult crime. All hideous crimes are considered adult crimes and punishment meted out the same way. Insanity and mental competency defenses are not recognized.

Drinking and Driving is not allowed in IMS. If a person drinks excess alcohol, that would be his/her problem. We will have treatment facilities available for alcohol addiction. But when the same person gets behind a wheel, that becomes Society's problem. If this causes an accident which results in death or serious injury to another person, the crime will result in mandatory removal from Society. The bar owners may be held financially liable.

If the innocent party escapes death or serious injury, the guilty persons should thank their lucky stars as death sentence will not be imposed. But the drunk driver will be heavily fined and then be under constant gaze of the authorities to make sure he/she does never drive again inebriated.

Talking on a cell phone as well as texting while driving fall under the same category as drinking and driving.

Causing an accident while driving on the wrong side will entail similar punishment.

Disintegration of two-parent families is one of the greatest long-term threats to the welfare and prosperity of any nation. Children raised by single mothers often fail in schools and commit crimes at a much higher rate than children raised by both parents. These children's social skills needed to become productive, self-sufficient adults are weaker on average. Single parent households are far more likely to be poor and dependent on government assistance. But more consequential than the risks to individual children is the cultural norm that is established of regarding fathers as mere instruments of procreation and not having equal responsibility for child-rearing. A society that fails to teach its young males that they are unambiguously responsible for their offspring will have a difficult task of inculcating other fundamental duties.

Therefore, producing a child and then walking away from the family is considered shirking from one's responsibility as a parent and is a severely punishable offense. Future wages will be garnished and will be used as child support. Second chances will be rarely given unless extenuating circumstances warrant them. We realize that each case is different and should be evaluated as such.

This does not mean that a single woman or a single man cannot have a child. If they are educated, well settled in life, able to provide for a child, then by all means, they can have a child or family. IMS is a progressive society and understands that this may bring happiness and stability to people's lives.

In closing this chapter, we will merely say to an individual; come to us (Society) before you commit a crime. We have all sorts of means available to help you. If you need a job, we will have something for you. If you are hungry, we will have soup kitchens throughout our land. If you need moral support or comfort, we have a gamut of programs available for you. We are a nurturing community. We are your family. In our Society, you are never alone. You are our loving Society's sons and daughters.

But once you commit an act of cruelty, we will show no mercy.

We envision IMS to be the safest nation on earth where nobody has to lock their doors, where a sixteen-year-old girl can go wherever she wants to go, alone in the middle of the night and come back home safe and sound. A police officer's job would be one of the easiest and safest of all.

Article 4

Society and White Collar Crimes

Society is equally tough on white collar crimes.

These crimes are generally committed by people who are educated and coming from relatively wealthy families rather than persons from uneducated class, bad neighborhoods or from unstable environments. Some crimes may be committed by organized crime syndicates.

Society defines white collar crimes as illegal or un-ethical acts that violate fiduciary responsibility of public trust committed by an individual or organization. They are usually committed during the course of legitimate occupational activity, by persons of respectable social status for personal or organizational gain. Mostly they are non-violent in nature. They may occur as frequently as other violent crimes.

It is important to note that Society does not perceive white collar crimes as any less harmful to the public at large. On the contrary, they are deemed more detrimental to the well-being of IsoloMetrik Society.

If a person commits financial fraud in which there are multiple victims who lose their life savings, or one that causes irreparable harm to a nation, it is a very serious crime. That person should be removed from the Society.

Ponzi schemes, identity thefts, credit card, social security, Medicare frauds are some of those crimes. Selling anything fraudulent to a vast populace would be another. Taking advantage of retirees, seniors, elders whose mental capacity may have been diminished might qualify.

Insider trading is forbidden. Cyber bulling and other digital crimes are also illegal.

Corporate behavior can be considered criminal and executives within the corporation can be held liable.

Each case should be judged separately. If these crimes do not deserve removal from Society, extremely heavy financial fines should be imposed. Fines should be such that it would make criminals a lot poorer depending on the severity of crime.

Article 5

Society and Judiciary

IsoloMetrik Society imposes term limits on judiciary also, both at the federal level as well as state or provincial level.

A 5 (or 9) person panel of appointed or elected judges will decide if a president or governor or for that matter any citizen has followed the constitution of IsoloMetrik Society. Each nation may decide if these judges will be appointed or elected. Also, number of judges (5 or 9) will depend on the size of each country, size of each province. Judges will act independently and not beholden to either the president, governor or any other legislative branch. They will be well compensated. The judges' tenure will be limited to a maximum of ten years regardless whether it coincides with election cycle, both at the provincial level as well as federal level. Majority opinion among the judges will be the final verdict. Matters adjudicated at the state level may be appealed once to the supreme court, provided the apex court accepts the case. Decision of the supreme court will be final. IsoloMetrik constitution will be so succinct that not much more elucidation will be needed to interpret it. Few issues that may need to be deliberated before the court should be disposed of very quickly. Most decisions should take no more than a week.

Now, above provision will make the apex court final arbiter of Society's constitution. In turn that may make courts the feared tyrants. They can swallow other branches of federal and provincial governments. We are well aware of this. To prevent this from happening, constitution provides for removal and/or impeachment of judges, for due causes (bribery, moral turpitude) by 60% of vote of representatives. Besides, the make-up of the court will change roughly every ten years anyway. So, the impact of over-zealous judiciary should be minimum.

Article 6

Society and Education

Human is a species existing among a myriad of all other animal species. It is the education that makes a human a human. It is education that instills self-confidence in a person. Education wakes the hidden talent and skills of a human being. And that in turn allows him to achieve his goals. Educated citizenry is vital for the progress of any nation. Without education there is darkness.

In IsoloMetrik Society, education is spelled with capital E. It is conducted on a WAR FOOTING. This includes, Pre-Kindergarten, K.G., Primary, Secondary as well as High School Education. Up to high school, education is compulsory and free. That means each IMS citizen will at least be a high school graduate, barring a few extremely handicapped ones.

In IMS, teachers themselves are highly educated and well trained. They are some of the highest paid public employees and tremendously motivated. They are provided all the tools necessary to mold a child. Since children are most impressionable in their infancy, early childhood development is very important. Therefore, up to primary schools, the classes should be as small as possible with teacher-student ratio of around 1:12 or 1:15. Of course, quality of teaching is far more important than the class size. If both can be achieved, great.

Each nation will have to determine what is the right teacher-student ratio depending on density of population and funds available. Mostly, funds should be available due to lack of crime, fair amount of taxation and good use of tax money collected. Schools should not start very early in the morning. Ideal starting time would be 8:30 or 9:00 a.m. Teenagers, due to their natural circadian rhythms, tend to fall asleep at night a couple of hours later than adults. Very early schooling starts mean a lot of sleep-deprived young ones and that is not a very healthy scenario. All schools should have before care and after care facilities. For those who cannot afford, free or subsidized nutritious breakfast and lunch should be provided as learning goes better with full stomachs.

Classrooms should become a very nurturing place for students, second only to their homes. Teachers should find classrooms to be heaven where they find total fulfillment in the profession they have chosen to devote their lives to.

Uniforms are required for students as they instill healthy discipline in schools. Uniforms also eliminate a chasm among rich and poor students. When they enter school premises, all students are equal regardless of their parents' monetary as well as social status. No one should be able to tell a child of a prince from a child of a pauper.

Public schools will be so good that private or home schooling, though allowed, will not be needed. Parochial schools will not be allowed in IMS.

Some may call this socialism. We vehemently disagree. We call it *Equalism*.

In IsoloMetrik Society, middle as well as high school curricula emphasize Math and Sciences as these subjects are essential to the progress of a nation. This does not mean that liberal arts are neglected. On the contrary, IMS believes that they are also necessary for a complete rounding of a student.

In some countries, young school girls are encouraged to participate in cheer-leading contests to entertain the spectators at many sporting events. It is a cultural thing. We understand that. Different nations have different cultures. And yet we cannot help but find it very demeaning to young women. It has a feel of having courtesans in medieval ages perform dances to entertain kings and queens. IMS frowns on such customs. The girls would be much better off spending their precious years either participating in sports itself or studying math and sciences. Nations as a whole will be much better off also. Same logic extends to professional sports.

Therefore, we ardently hope that cheer-leading will not be encouraged by coaches, teachers and especially, parents.

In IMS, educating a child is a collaborative process between teachers and parents. There are regular meetings with each child's parents to appraise them of their child's progress. Input from parents is always encouraged. There may be a variety of reasons why some parents may not be able to participate in such a process. They may not be literate enough, they may be poor, the families may be broken, whatever. Not to worry. Society will act as their benevolent parent.

Teachers are hired to teach in the classroom. As such, they should not have to worry about their own safety or any other kind of disturbance from the students. Discipline must be maintained at all times. If need be, classrooms can be constantly watched. Offending students should be counseled by experts in the field. Other disciplinary steps should be taken if deemed necessary. Of course, parents must be informed and they should take an active role in finding a solution. In short, all the steps that need to be taken, will be taken to remedy the malady. If everything fails, the offending students will be considered incorrigible. They will be barred from the classroom.

Again, Society will take no pleasure in it and this will be done with a sincere sigh of regret and failure on the part of the Society. Barred students will be the responsibility of their parents for their behavior. Parents should make sure that these youngsters not fall into a life of crime.

When children have to grow up in a hurry in any country, that is an ominous sign that that country is on the brink of collapse. IsoloMetrik Society is very proud of the fact that children will remain children until they are not children any more due to the progression that nature intended.

Article 7

Society and Libraries

IsoloMetrik Society considers libraries temples of learning, second only to class-rooms.

Whereas class-rooms are formal, structured form of education, libraries are non-formal unsystematic form of education. Class-room education is somewhat time bound and rigid, while libraries offer free flowing learning.

In IMS, libraries become welfare centers, providing useful services to nearby communities by fostering education, promoting culture, recreation and dissemination of information to all sections of society. They not only carry all kinds of books but also provide invaluable services to citizens such as storytelling for children, after-school programs, playgrounds, language learning seminars, art and craft activities, sundry workshops and much more. Critical services that libraries provide to individuals and families at the lower end of economic spectrum will serve as a lifeline.

Society considers investments in libraries as complimentary to investments in human capital. They are one of the few places that provide common ground to all citizens. In fact, library programs will encourage parents to play a much bigger role in their children's literacy development.

In IsoloMetrik Society, libraries act not only as educational and literacy agents, but they play a considerable role in nations' economic development by providing all kind of business resources and a forum for business communities to get together to discuss economic as well as business concerns.

Libraries will strengthen democracies of nations by providing civic societies with education programs and by disseminating necessary information to develop a well-versed electorate.

Through open access Internet facilities, they can help with voter registration and even serve as polling stations. They can also be used to reach out to politically unmotivated citizens, publicize party positions, solicit feedback, new ideas and new members. They can and will provide and exchange vital information needed for dialogue that public needs. So, people can make decisions about common concerns and ensure government accountability.

Free access to information is vital to the issue of human rights. Along with physical freedom, intellectual freedom is a basic human right. Deprivation of this right leads to autocratic governance. In IsoloMetrik Society, libraries provide this free access.

IMS is well aware that without libraries, past is just a blur and future would be bleak.

No library in IMS will suffer from paucity of funds. Qualified librarians will be decently paid disseminators of knowledge. Philanthropists will be highly encouraged to donate to libraries.

Article 8

Society and Health Care

Health is wealth.

This is not only true for individuals; it is true for countries also. A healthy nation is a wealthy nation.

Health care is important to all societies because people fall sick, accidents and emergencies do arise, hospitals are needed to diagnose, treat and cure different types of ailments and diseases. People's aspirations and desires cannot be fulfilled without longer, healthier, happier lives.

IMS defines health care as the diagnosis, treatment, prevention and management of disease, illness, injury and preservation of physical and mental well-being of its citizens. It also feels that it is a basic right for all of its citizens to have reasonable and timely access to decent health care regardless of income and/or personal status.

To that end, IsoloMetrik Society broadly endorses the concept of Universal Health Care as well as Single Payer System (SPS).

SPS is not run by the government. It is publicly financed with revenue coming from fair amount of taxation as well as premium based on income plus accumulated assets. Under this system, every citizen gets a health care card and can go to any doctor or hospital. We recommend some type of nominal co-pay so that citizens don't run to the clinic for every little ailment like slight spell of cough or cold. But there will be no rationing of health care. The biggest advantage here is the bargaining power the government has due to very large number of citizens insured. So, if a hospital or a doctor says I will charge 'X' amount for this operation or this treatment, government can come back and counter that offer with lesser amount. If the hospital or the doctor does not want to accept that lesser offer, government has the option of going somewhere else. Thus, there is a strong chance of citizens getting reasonably priced care. This problem of haggling over the costs can be eliminated if the cost of each service is pre-determined by panels of doctors and skilled administrators, so nobody feels cheated or violated. And that is exactly what the Society intends to do.

Of course, each action has its own unintended ramifications. In some countries, insurance industry is all too powerful. They dictate many medical decisions, payments to the doctors, how long a patient may stay in the hospital, what medications may be prescribed, etc. etc. Single Payer System may destroy, or at least hobble, the insurance industry. It may throw many middle men and women out of jobs. It may increase unemployment and may have negative effect on the economy in the short run. But Society also understands that things have a way of settling down. Insurance industry will reinvent itself and like a chameleon, emerge into another strong industry. Displaced workers will find other suitable positions either on their own or through retraining.

The key to success of SPS is good governance, proper accountability of expenditure and as little wastage as possible.

In many countries, malpractice lawsuits are quite common and routinely filed. This tremendously increases the cost of medical practice and is generally passed on to the patients. IsoloMetrik Society does not allow filing of such lawsuits through private for-profit lawyers. This does not mean that Society accepts gross negligence by hospitals and/or doctors. Patients are welcome to file complaints if they feel they have been grossly mistreated. IMS will have panels of highly qualified independent doctors as well as skilled administrators ready to examine these complaints. If gross negligence is found, patients will be fairly compensated and suitable action will be taken against the hospitals/doctors.

Vaccination of newborns and children is very important to prevent spread of preventable diseases. These vaccinations have been touted by majority of scientists and doctors as one of the greatest achievements of modern medicine. They have increased the life span of citizens in all countries. We do understand that some parents may have concerns over safety of these vaccines. Very tiny percentage of children may have suffered adverse allergic reactions after vaccinations or their health might have regressed. And yet, no causal connections have been established between vaccinations and catastrophic illnesses such as autism. Whereas the benefits of vaccinations are just too numerous to be put at risk.

Another issue is herd immunity. No body lives in a bubble. If one child is not inoculated, that child can spread the diseases to many. They may unwittingly bring back preventable diseases that have already been wiped out. If close to hundred percent of people get vaccinated, it builds a so called hermetically sealed wall to protect that community against preventable diseases. This is the only protection some very young and some very old people have who cannot be vaccinated due to severe medical conditions.

Freedom of choice for parents as well as individuals does not apply when it comes to vaccinating the entire population. Good of the nation becomes paramount. So, no exemption is provided for personal or religious beliefs. There will only be medical exemption.

Finally, this concept of universal health care comes with a tremendous amount of cost associated with it. Nations with dual burden of exploding population and meagre resources may find it difficult to even think about it, leave alone implementing it. We totally understand the dilemma. So, each country has to decide how deep it can go in implementing this system.

Article 9

Society and Work Ethic

IsoloMetrik Society endorses *protestant* work ethic.

Citizens of IMS are not only expected to work hard to finish an assigned task but work diligently throughout the entire process of finishing that task well, no matter how much time and effort they may have to expend. This is how Society loosely defines protestant work ethic.

We do not wish to elaborate a whole lot further as most people understand this concept. We merely wish to state that this work ethic will be inculcated in our youth at an early stage in their lives. Students at the middle school level will be instilled with the idea that good work ethic is very important not only for their own development but also for the progress of their nation.

Parents should be encouraged to play an important role in this process so that their children get into the habit of working hard, thereby giving them a tremendous jump start on life.

Just because Society exhorts its citizens to work hard, that does not mean they should work all year long without enjoying some time off. All workers should take vacation days to get away from the rat race, spend time with their families and recharge their batteries. In fact, employers should actively encourage their employees to take at least three to four weeks off a year and come back to work fresh, in body, mind and spirit. This would benefit all concerned as workers will be more productive. Same goes for executives also. It will have an added benefit of imparting humility, as it reminds every one that no one is irreplaceable.

Article 10

Society and UBI

In principle, we endorse the concept of Universal Basic Income for developed nations.

Every day, there is news about innovations in the field of artificial intelligence and industry automation. More and more jobs previously done by humans are being performed by robots; faster, better and with greater efficiency. Even though the day when robots will take over all of the jobs humans perform seems far away, the number of tasks learned by robots is astounding. And it is increasing with each passing year.

This gives rise to a simple and yet, profound question: what will humans do when robots take over all of their jobs? It is a given that money and consumption are the main driving forces of every country's economy. But where and how will people get money if they have no jobs?

The answer may lie in a concept known as Universal Basic Income. IMS defines it as universal or unconditional sum of money given to each citizen of a nation by the government, without individuals having to work for it. It is not the same as minimum income or living wage. The key word here is *unconditional,* which means that regardless of a person's labor contribution, he or she receives a fixed income sufficient enough for food, clothing and shelter. The sum will be different for each country as cost of living as well as standard of living is totally different for each nation. UBI possesses several important characteristics. Every person, by right of birth, receives it regardless of social or financial status. It is not a one-time payment. It is given monthly or annually. It should be given in cash, not in the form of goods and services. Every individual receiving UBI should be able to decide for themselves how and what they want to spend the money on. Sum should be barely enough to live. UBI is supposed to not only increase the quality of life of a country's citizens but also reduce or eliminate bureaucracy as well as scales of governmental control over people's eligibility and behavior. That is why many people on both sides of the spectrum, *right-leaning* as well as *left-*

leaning, favor this concept. According to them, UBI is neither *left-leaning* nor *right-leaning*; it is *forward-leaning*. They all see it as a great way to fix a large number of problems associated with social safety net that most countries have. It is like eliminating poverty with a stroke of a pen.

IsoloMetrik Society believes that this somewhat utopian idea of UBI is realistic and doable, at least, for western civilization. This is not socialism. Absolutely not. Far from it. Right now, only people with money have a voice in the market place. Those who have money to buy bread have a say in deciding how much bread should be baked. People who have no money, cannot buy bread. They are not counted and bypassed by the market system. By providing basic income to every citizen, society gives voice to every citizen in deciding how the market behaves. It is a win-win for the market and the nation. It is a good way to improve capitalism and even democracy as every citizen has a vote when they purchase goods and services they need or want. Providing more income security to the struggling working class would not only create a more equitable society, it would also increase spending, boosting the economic growth. Besides, UBI is a great way to recognize the importance of unpaid work; housewives will be paid for house work, young adults paid for caring for their elderly and/or sick parents.

Some may say the greatest disadvantage facing implementation of UBI is that it will be a tremendous disincentive to work. At first glance, it may seem to be true. However, we need to look a little deeper. When we do that, this fear of *no body wanting to work* does not hold much water. Surely, there will be a small percentage, who may decide not to work at all. But the thing to remember is that UBI offers amount that is barely enough for food, clothing and shelter; it is not enough to offer finer things in life. And most people would like finer things for their families, for their children. This can only be achieved by supplementing UBI through work. Another important thing to keep in mind is that work is not just what people do to earn a living. It offers status. It offers contacts to the outside world. It offers structure and stability in life. It offers social and psychological anchor. It offers certain rhythm to one's life. UBI can never replace it. Thus, most citizens would prefer to work to augment their basic income. Exploitation of workers will be non-existent as they will have ability to say "no" to poor working conditions as well as paltry wages. They may work fewer hours rather than putting in long hours, which may not be a bad thing. It should increase productivity as well as innovations. More time spent with family and children would be healthy for any society and lead to happier lives.

Another objection some may raise is that UBI would redefine relationship between individuals, families, communities and the state by giving government the role of a provider. It would render self-reliance moot. Adults have certain responsibilities, endowed by thousands of years of culture, of providing for their families, raising children, educating them, caring for their elderly parents. The list can go on. These duties are fundamental to any society's character. They establish terms of relationships, the scope and the role of individuals in any civil society. This objection to redefinition of relationship between the governments and their subjects is valid to a certain extent. But most of the civilized countries redefine these relationships anyway by implementing all of the programs incorporated in their safety nets. Some to a lesser degree, some a little more.

Now the most important question of them all. What will be the cost of implementing the idea of Universal Basic Income and how will any nation pay for it?

It goes without saying that costs would be huge. But isn't the cost of all of the safety net programs that most countries have, not very high? In fact, IsoloMetrik Society feels that by eliminating all these current, hugely wasteful means-testing programs full of unnecessary bureaucracy, UBI may be affordable as everything else will be defunded. Any shortfall could be made up by imposing value added tax or carbon footprint tax or general consumption tax or any other combination of taxes in addition to regular income tax for those in higher income brackets, making sure that such taxes do not chock off productivity and innovations.

On final analysis, IMS feels that implementing the idea of Universal Basic Income is doable for rich, developed countries. Income should be given to adults only, not the children so that family planning is not thwarted. We need to keep in mind that anything given to public is very difficult to eliminate later on. So, citizens must be told that UBI will be implemented for five years and then it automatically expires unless renewed by elected officials. Budget deficits are not allowed. Society should request rich citizens, earning well above the basic income, to return UBI sum back to treasury on a voluntary basis. IMS will implement a scheme that would make it very easy to do so. Some will return the money or agree not to take it in the first place. Many more may follow. That should help lower the cost of the program.

For countries over burdened by exploding population and meagre resources, UBI is not doable and they should not even think about it. Just make sure population does not starve.

Article 11

Society and Living Wage

In absence of UBI, we endorse the concept of Living Wage for a working person.

It is an economic reform movement that has become an important public policy issue. While there cannot be a single definition of what constitutes a living wage, IMS defines it as wage that lifts working class families above the poverty line and allows them to sustain a semblance of decent monetary life. Obviously, the amount would be different for different nations but basically it should provide proper nutrition, health care, housing, clothing and transportation for the workers and their families.

We strongly disagree with those who may say this is socialism. We consider this as *prudent capitalism*.

Income and income distribution is an important social determinant of health. Suicide rates and onset of many diseases such as diabetes and heart ailments are significantly more prevalent amongst low income families.

Though, the effort to help the poor and reduce the income gap is laudable, we do understand that it comes at a tremendous cost. For many under-developed, poor and over-populated nations with finite means and infinite needs, these costs can be overwhelming. Businesses may also flinch at the higher costs and hire fewer workers, thereby increasing unemployment. So, these kinds of social policies for those countries should be examined very carefully as they might have prohibitive ramifications. Each nation has to decide for itself whether establishing a living wage would be feasible or not as long as they have established a *minimum* wage.

For rich, developed nations, such high economic cost considerations pale in comparison to moral and social high grounds. IsoloMetrik Society sees no compelling reason for not enacting a living wage law. Eventually it will lead to a happier, healthier, more productive citizenry.

Article 12

Society and Media

IsoloMetrik Society is well aware that one of the most important ingredients of democracy is the existence of free and fearless media. Voice of the press is the voice of the people and therefore censoring the media is equivalent to suppressing people's voice. The very survival of democracy depends on this freedom of press.

Press plays a very positive and constructive role in any democracy. It keeps people *informed*. By the same token, it keeps government abreast of ordinary people's problems, difficulties, hopes and aspirations so that the government does not function in a vacuum. Thus, it acts as a bridge between the government and the governed.

That is why, in IMS, press and all other kinds of media enjoy full freedom of expression without fear of government's vendetta. It is not subservient to the whims and fancies of powerful government bureaucrats. It investigates official lapses and misdoings and makes them public.

On the other hand, Society believes that primary duty of the media is objective reporting of news in a calm and dispassionate manner. Just because freedom of the press is guaranteed in IMS' constitution, that is not a license for character assassination. Mudslinging, blackmailing, rumor spreading and any other kind of *yellow journalism* is simply not permitted.

Society is especially tough on Fake News. It has stringent laws to prevent dissemination of fake news. Punishment is very severe for violation of these laws. In most egregious cases, heavy financial penalties may be imposed.

Paparazzi are not allowed to hound celebrities. Society feels they should engage in more productive line of work to make a living.

In IsoloMetrik Society, media is not considered an enemy of the government. On the contrary, it actively solicits media's help in promoting a healthy and robust climate. A vigilant, fearless and responsible media is an important pillar of strength of our Society.

Article 13

Society and Guns

In IsoloMetrik Society, no one has a constitutional right to bear arms except, of course, the Armed Forces and Law Enforcement Officers. These officers will be very well trained and sensitive to the populace in general. They will be fully accountable for their use of force. Policy of mandatory dash cam will be implemented, so that officers' conduct can be public knowledge.

We realize that many people in many countries are outdoors men and women with a passion for hunting. We say *fine*. Society has no problem with any law-abiding citizen owning hunting rifles or for that matter any legitimate weapon used for hunting.

But nobody hunts with handguns or Uzi machine guns or AK47. These weapons are manufactured with only one intention in mind. To kill as many humans as possible, as quickly as possible. They are weapons of war and war only.

Cost of senseless gun violence for any nation is very huge. And though substantial, it is not just financial. The heartaches, the grief, the anger of losing a loved one, loss of innocence are all immeasurable byproducts.

Every nation has a duty to enact sensible gun laws. There is no easy access to guns for citizens of IMS. Thorough background checks are required for anyone wanting to purchase a hunting rifle so as to weed out buyers who should not be buying any kind of weapon. A permit is required and each and every gun owned by a private citizen is registered.

Countries in which guns proliferate, private citizens are allowed to keep a gun at home for self-defense. But it has to be registered and licensed. Ultimately, though, goal is to make sure that guns are not ubiquitous in any nation.

Maximum punishment for possessing an unlicensed or unregistered weapon is extremely severe. In such cases, they may face intense surveillance. We do realize that each case is unique and merits its own evaluation. If they possess unlicensed weapons, checking their background, their education level, their upbringing, their temperament, their intent, their economic status and meting out punishment accordingly is not considered discriminatory in the eyes of the Society. This may raise a hue and cry that it discriminates against minorities and the dispossessed. These citizens may feel that they are being watched more intensely or more often than others.

That may be true but it is perfectly legal and necessary.

There is no other ulterior motive behind this policy except to reduce and ultimately eliminate gun violence.

That is all.

Article 14

Society and Economic Considerations

Every nation has adopted its own economic system. We have keenly observed them all and have concluded that market economy has produced the best results. Socialism and communism have done nothing but impoverished its people.

Strong property rights, free press, honest bureaucracies, rule of law, relatively free trade, fierce competition among manufacturers and industries are the hallmarks of IsoloMetrik Society. This does not mean that government has no role in directing the economy but its role should be limited. It should not choke the industries with unnecessary and over bearing regulations. It is best to leave the people alone, empowering them to do what they do well; work hard, innovate and generate wealth.

Just because we favor market economy, we are not totally against redistribution of income. In many countries, the gap in income is so huge amongst their populace so as to become unconscionable. Such wide disparity among the haves and have nots, breeds instability and is a sign of a declining nation. It also creates public health crisis and a greater array of social problems. When top 1 or 2 percent own more assets than the bottom 90 percent, it frays the entire social fabric of a nation. In fact, it cleaves a nation. So, addressing this inequality becomes one of the top priorities of any administration. Under these conditions, some redistribution of income in the form of higher taxation of the rich, would not only be justified but wise.

Hundreds of books have been written on this subject. We do not even pretend to understand the intricacies of these monetary systems. We will leave detailed explanation and administration of monetary policies to the more erudite as long as it is within the framework of free market system.

Article 15

Society and Taxation

Taxes are the price we all have to pay if we want a civilized society.

They are essential for our social, civil, political institutions and for security of life and property. Rightful taxation is the price for social order. It is not to be wantonly levied on the citizens. It can only be levied for benefits it confers.

IMS requires that taxation system should be simple and transparent, low in complexity as well as layers. Collection process should be streamlined.

All nations are different and they have different needs. Society does not recommend any particular tax system. A country may adopt progressive tax rate, flat tax rate, rate based on consumption of goods or whatever else that may suit the nation and its people. However, any tax system chosen should not overburden the poor. It must be equitable, efficient, well accounted for and tax dollars collected expended to achieve economic growth and development for the benefit of nation's citizenry. It is also alright to harness tax dollars to bridge the gap somewhat between the very rich and the very poor as extreme disparity in income is a troubling sign of instability of a country.

It is best to leave creation and implementation of any tax system to the experts of each nation.

Article 16

Society and Budgetary Considerations

IMS believes deficits do matter. If budget deficits are small, positive effects may outweigh any negative effects. But small deficits have a way to invariably turn into overwhelmingly large deficits which can easily decimate a nation. Huge deficits can contribute to price instability. If government resorts to financing this deficit by printing money, it can lead to runaway inflation. If government issues debt, competition with businesses and other individuals for investment dollars results, increasing the cost of borrowing to finance productive investments in private sector. Budget deficits can only be funded by additional increases in the level of national debt, which will place an undue burden on future generations to repay such debt. A weak fiscal position can weaken government's ability to provide security for life and property rights. Being over leveraged makes it that much more difficult to borrow in the face of any security crisis or other unforeseen catastrophe. Most importantly, the government may lose its role as a credible, legitimate governing entity.

Public debt is thus one of the greatest dangers facing any country. So, need to be financially solvent will always be necessary.

That is why IMS requires that not only budgets of cities, municipalities, states or provinces be balanced every year but the budget of a whole nation must also be balanced every year. Wars and other catastrophic events are not allowed to be exceptions because once the debt of a country is out of control, that debt becomes perpetual. What we recommend is temporary or one-time levy of special war-tax or catastrophe-tax that should automatically disappear once the event does not warrant such a levy.

Article 17

Society and Regulation of Businesses

IMS understands that businesses play a very important role in every aspect of a nation's life. Citizens' standard of living, life style, education, cultural standards are all determined by businesses. So, it is a given that they should be governed by some sort of regulations.

The question is how much regulation is enough? It is a difficult task to strike a balance between regulations that will enhance the quality of life of citizenry and a glut of regulations that will hamper businesses, create artificial barriers and chock off innovations, which in turn diminish quality of life of people.

Sure, the government should promulgate regulations that would ensure workplace safety, reduce pollution, improve areas for the handicapped etc. No one likes to walk into a store where conditions are unsanitary, food labels are misleading, out of date drugs and medicine are sold. Government regulations help in breaking up monopolies, thereby increasing competition and lowering prices for the consumers. Regulations disallowing businesses to discriminate against race, gender, religion etc., are a good thing as they give fair chances to all potential employees to find work. It goes without saying that releasing carbon into the atmosphere or dumping chemical waste into lakes and rivers are, of course, very harmful, both environmentally as well as for spreading of diseases and should be strictly regulated.

It is important to remember that bureaucracies, once established, are virtually impossible to abolish. In many countries, a lot of bureaus and agencies have been created to regulate some things that no longer need to be regulated. Many of these regulations and programs no longer serve their purposes or they are hopelessly outdated. Granted, initially they were established for efficient functioning of businesses but after a while they become obstructive, which make businesses inefficient. Many of a nation's economic problems stem from the fact that a large proportion of economic decisions are made through the political process rather than the market process.

To solve these dilemmas, IsoloMetrik Society will enact most of the regulations and establish agencies and bureaus with an expiry date. One or two cycles of elections should be plenty. If they are still found to be useful, they can be easily extended by an act of legislation following a careful study.

This way, a flood of new and burdensome regulations can be drastically curtailed, which in turn, will help the economy flourish.

Of course, every country is different. Every country has its own culture, its own environment, its own unique jumble of people. So, each nation has to set its own business regulations best suited to its needs.

Article 18

Society and Pensions

IsoloMetrik Society does not allow implementation of any kind of pension plans. It does not provide pensions to its employees nor does it allow any governmental organization to provide pensions to their employees.

In fact, private corporations are also banned from providing pensions to their employees.

Permit us to elaborate.

We have seen all the ills associated with pension plans. Pensions are liabilities that must be met sometime in the future. Most of these plans are inadequately funded. Nobody knows what the future holds or what the future costs will be. A company may be highly profitable today. In twenty, thirty, fifty years from now, who knows? It may be losing money, it may have to file for bankruptcy, it may go out of existence. Government organizations have fared even worse. Promises of future benefits cannot be satisfactorily sustained.

Instead, IMS believes in paying employees well in the present where circumstances are known. In fact, Society insists that a portion of each employee's salary should be earmarked for their retirement. We suggest anywhere between ten to twenty percent must be reserved for this purpose and this should be paid on top of a base salary. Employees cannot spend that money and it should be invested on their behalf for future consumption. This is their deferred compensation. This is their Social Security. Each nation may decide when to tax this money or not to tax it at all. If in certain years the profit is huge, companies may increase their contribution toward this goal.

Article 19

Society and Patriotism

We realize, this is a nebulous field. Each nation has to define for itself what the word patriotism means and how to interpret it. A simple definition of love of or devotion to one's country is profoundly inadequate.

Some utterances may be obvious. If a person says he hates his country and wants to blow it up and means it, that person is undoubtedly unpatriotic. If a person passes confidential or critical information to the enemy, that is an unpatriotic act. Committing treason would definitely be unpatriotic. All these acts, if egregious, should result in maximum punishment.

However, IMS is strongly against so called blind, uneducated, jingoistic patriotism. Society encourages citizens to speak up and even rebel peacefully if they think government has exceeded its boundaries. It believes in free speech and invites exchange of ideas. After all, what is Society? It cannot be separated from its citizens. Society and its citizens are one and the same; a single inseparable entity. Just because people criticize their government, it does not make them unpatriotic. In fact, they may be more patriotic. Society feels that if people work to ensure that all nations live up to their collective moral and ethical values at home as well as abroad and be critical of their countries when they do not, that is true patriotism.

Defining patriotism in multi-cultural, multi-religion, multi-ethnic countries is also a big challenge as back-bones of social unity may be very dissimilar.

Exploitation of bandwagon or faux patriotism to serve government's interests, to justify war, to commit injustice against others, to manipulate the populace is frowned upon in IsoloMetrik Society.

IMS allows national flag to be desecrated if citizens do it as a sign of protest against some of government's policies as long as such protests are otherwise peaceful. Destruction of property and looting is not permitted.

A three-person (or five-person, depending on the size and vastness of a country) panel of highly trained individuals is set up to judge if the action can be considered unpatriotic and the severity of it. Majority opinion of these judges will determine guilt or innocence and the level of seriousness of it.

This may be done at the local or provincial stage but must then be swiftly reaffirmed by the national panel.

Article 20

Society and Civility

IMS has observed that as human race is advancing in many fields, civility is declining at an alarming rate. We recognize that there is a state of uncivil discourse in many nations. We have no intention of just becoming accustomed to it.

We do realize that part of the reason may be advances in technology, hectic lifestyle, pressures of raising a family etc. etc. Religion, race, gender, family, they all play a role in this decline. Whatever the reasons may be, it does not justify rude, crude behavior towards other human beings. People should understand that simply winning arguments is not very useful. Respecting other people leads to goodwill. Continued cooperation is better than a frowned consent. For this to happen, one must present one's opinions modestly with due regard to others' feelings. Instead of anger and arrogance, politeness encourages common ground. In these troubled times, politeness offers an escape from bitterness that may engulf people otherwise. Doing the right thing and being polite are not contradictory. In fact, they go together.

IMS does not accept insolence easily. The old adage "Treat others exactly the way you would like to be treated'' still very much holds true.

Television and movies are big reason why people act so rudely. Children think that whatever they see on the screen is the way everybody is supposed to act. Boys think that if they want to be tough like the boy they saw on the screen, they better behave like him, which is usually manner-less. Girls think that if they want to be beautiful and popular, they have to dress and act just as rudely as the girl they just saw on the screen. Internet also brings plenty of uncivilized pomposity to this arena.

TV shows and movies that dumb down a nation are strictly controlled and, in some cases, prohibited by the Society. Some may say this is dictatorship or authoritarianism. May be. Though we would like to call it noble intervention and is simply the right thing to do.

Society frowns on people throwing garbage on the road, spitting on the street, sticking gum underneath a sitting bench in the park etc. etc. Extremely heavy fines will be imposed on such uncouth behavior.

There are stringent laws on the books against anti-social behavior and these laws will be enforced.

Best way to make a nation civil is to inculcate middle and high school children in civic lessons. *Be mindful of others* is the most important phrase they will be taught. That is all it takes to make any country civil. We understand it is a long, arduous process, but it is still the best way.

A civil society is not a *cowardly* society. Civility is strength, not weakness.

Article 21

Society and Corporations

IsoloMetrik Society understands that a declining middle class of a nation is a sure sign of decline of the nation itself. IMS therefore is determined not to allow that to happen to their Society.

In IsoloMetrik Society, big public corporations have a duty to perform aside from making profits for their shareholders.

They have to anchor their communities in which they exist. They should become a beating heart of these communities.

By this, we mean, their immediate locality should become more or less, a company town. Company executives should live nearby where most of the workers reside. They should shop at the same grocery stores, same department stores, go to the same religious institutions. Executives should attend their employees' family weddings as well as funerals. Workers do not have to be paid huge salaries but depending on profits, corporations should organize picnics, games, fairs, among other things. Children of the executives and workers should go to the same public schools, mingle and play in the same playgrounds, swim in the same swimming pools. This, of course, does not preclude people from having their own little playgrounds and swimming pools in their backyards if they so choose.

Each company locality (town) should be well planned. They should have distinctive, safe footpaths as well as bicycle lanes. Auto drivers should be amply cautioned to be extra careful where people ride bikes and children play.

Most people need a larger, wider bond than just their immediate families. They also need a strong holistic protector. A large corporation can and should become just that. Who else is better suited to lend a helping hand to workers and protect them against vicissitudes of life?

This is not socialism. Far from it. This is wise policy. This is what we call, the epitome of free enterprise. Workers should have a sense of belonging. They should be looking forward to go to work the next day. They should feel lucky that they are working for a benevolent corporation. Frankly, the executives should feel the same way too.

And this would do it. A happy work force is a productive work force.

Article 22

Society and Prostitution

Prostitution is legal in IsoloMetrik Society.

We are not going to delve deeply into the subject matter of prostitution nor discuss whatever virtues and vices it may have. We are not debating whether it is moral or immoral, whether it is beneficial or detrimental to any nation. Maybe it is an immoral act, which goes against ethics of most cultures and religions. Maybe it is a license to be promiscuous. Maybe it destroys families and brings about social instability. Maybe it threatens the institution of marriage itself. Maybe it exploits a sex worker and spreads sexually transmitted diseases.

All we are saying is that it is the oldest profession in the world. As long as civilization has existed, prostitution has not been far behind. Take any country in the world where prostitution is illegal and you will find a thriving sex trade. It cannot be stopped. As long as there is demand, there will be a supply. And experience, logic and common sense tells us that there will always be a demand.

Since it cannot be stopped, the trade should be de-criminalized. It should be legalized and properly regulated. It will weaken those who exploit illegal business of prostitution. Pimps and organized crimes will be reduced or eliminated. Rapes, murders and beating of sex workers will be reduced. Regulating the business of prostitution will create a safer, healthier work environment for those who are offering their services and for those who pay for them.

In IsoloMetrik Society, certain area will be designated in each city as a *Red-Light* district. Business of prostitution may be conducted only in that area. No person can be forced in to prostitution. Minimum age is twenty-one to engage in this business. All sex workers will have to undergo regular health examinations. Ample precautions will be taken to make sure that most feared sexually transmitted diseases are not contracted or widely spread.

Business of prostitution and sex workers will be taxed just like any other business.

Article 23

Society and Drugs

In IsoloMetrik Society, Drugs are legal.

Towards this, our argument is simple.

Prohibition of alcohol did not work. Selling, distribution and consumption of alcohol had to be made legal. Same for drugs. There is an obscene amount of money in illegal drug trade. Whenever there is this kind of money involved, people will find a way to trade. As is the case with any illegal trade, this one also promotes crime and corruption. Governments have to spend huge amount of their limited resources to fight this scourge instead of devoting these resources towards the betterment of their citizenry. Many of the victims in war on drugs are innocent bystanders. They are the ones who suffer robberies, theft, muggings, murders, drive-by-shootings, gang wars. Some of them may be victims of addicts who are trying to support their habits but many more fall victims because, as mentioned above, huge amount of limited resources must be spent to try to control these drugs, which in turn, does not leave enough resources to fight other crimes.

War on illegal drugs is unwinnable. We cannot put it any more succinctly than that.

Legalization of drugs will take unconscionable profit out of equation. And if IsoloMetrik Society knows anything at all, it knows human nature. No profit, no trade. Black market in drug sales will be a thing of the past. Violent illegal drug dealers would be driven out of business.

Undesirable and unwanted consequence of legalization of drugs, will inevitably be, abuse of drugs. It is possible that legalization of drugs may increase its usage and create more addicts. But they will be softer addicts, not criminals. Drugs will be a lot cheaper. So, they will not have to rob or mug anyone. Drugs will be manufactured by reputable firms and sold in liquor stores or pharmacies, so fewer people will die of overdoses and tainted drugs. Doctors will not be allowed to prescribe pain killers unless it is absolutely medically necessary; and that too in limited quantities.

IMS treats drugs just like alcohol. Both will be regulated pretty much the same way. Selling drugs to minors will be prohibited. Pregnant mothers will be counseled to stay off the drugs. There will be effective system of prenatal care available. Society will have plenty of drug addiction treatment centers staffed with expert, knowledgeable people.

There will be sufficient funding for *Drugoholics Anonymous* along with Alcoholics Anonymous.

Article 24

Society and Obesity

Obesity has become a major, major health issue among many adults and children all across our world. It affects not only physical health, but emotional health as well. Many morbidly obese people become loners and have a low self-esteem. It is one of the causes of early deaths every year. It is a leading contributor of type-2 diabetes, high blood pressure, heart disease, cancer and countless other health ailments. It is becoming a threat for a global epidemic and the crisis cannot be clearer.

There are many causes for this disease. Genetics may be at the root of it. Other factors like eating habits, food preparation, sedentary lifestyle, transportation may also play a role. Culture plays a huge role. Family history, ethnicity, smoking, environment are also a big part of the problem. Where convenience, ease and quick fixes seem appropriate for any situation, such expeditious lifestyle supports our obese world. Low socioeconomic status influences patterns of eating due to *food insecurity* syndrome. It restricts access to healthy nourishment linking poverty to soaring obesity.

Obesity's costs to a nation's economy is staggering. It stifles businesses and organizations that stimulate jobs and growth. There is added medical and prescription drugs costs. Employers lose inordinate amount in productivity due to employee absenteeism. Disability and unemployment benefits costs rise. These are the bills that no nation can afford to pay.

Nor should they.

Time has now come not for just words but for action. Food industry needs to change. Individuals have to accept accountability. Transformation is imperative. Government has to step in.

IsoloMetrik Society knows it and is ready to step in.

There is a direct correlation to eating more calories than what your body needs and can burn and gaining weight. In other words, over-eating causes obesity. Sugary soft drinks are also responsible for spreading this disease. So, Society strongly discourages serving large glasses of such drinks. The sole aim of IMS is welfare of its citizens. And what is better welfare of its people than a chance to reduce obesity of a nation?

In IsoloMetrik Society, everybody has a role to play in reducing this scourge. It starts with educating middle and high school children about the scale and magnitude of this crisis. Since lack of exercise is one of the main culprits, regular physical activity and daily PE classes are implemented in schools. This not only reduces childhood obesity but also improves their academic performance. Social media and marketing campaigns are used to elicit help of general public. They are encouraged to play a sport, join a fitness class and generally say goodbye to a sedentary lifestyle.

Article 25

Society and Family Planning

A nation that does not have adequate family planning, will invariably descend into a state of penury; some a lot sooner, some later.

So, in IsoloMetrik Society, family planning is mandatory. Religion is not allowed to interfere in this matter.

Before we delve any further on the issue, we want to state unequivocally that IsoloMetricians do not like abortions. Nobody should like abortions. With proper family planning and early education, there should not be a whole lot of abortions in the Society any way. However, if they are needed under any circumstances, safe abortion on demand is a law of the land. For those who cannot afford it, it will be provided free of charge. This will mostly involve highly over-populated and poor countries.

Fetal tissues, embryos and anything else that can be harvested to help the living beings as well as medical research must be donated to further the science.

Population explosion is one of the biggest problems facing human race today. It will always outstrip food production, thus perpetually condemning overwhelming majority of humans to malnutrition. Most countries in this world have extremely limited resources to spend on basic necessities of life for their people. Rapid rise in population can put tremendous pressure on providing basic services such as food, shelter, clothing, education, employment etc.

With phenomenal advances in science, technology, medicine and health care, people are living longer. If birth rate does not decline commensurately, most of the developmental plans of nations have very little chance of succeeding. Millions of people will be deprived of even the most basic of services. Gulf between rich and poor will keep on widening. The entire social fabric will be torn apart. That is a recipe for trouble.

Rich keep getting richer while poor keep producing more children is a saying that rings true. Having too many children is a burden for most families. Parents cannot pay proper attention to all their children if there are too many. Some of them may suffer nutritional, emotional and all other kind of deficiencies. They may not grow up to be robust, productive citizens of the country.

That is why, IMS does not hesitate in taking drastic steps to facilitate family planning.

First step is to inculcate middle and high school children to the concept of family planning, to the *two children* norm.

Free contraceptives will be made available, along with sterilization, tubal legation etc. Maternal and child health care, pre-natal care, nutrition, family welfare programs will be given importance. Financial and other kind of incentives may be offered to encourage family planning. Society will spare no cost towards this goal.

Teenage pregnancies are not allowed. More on that in later chapter.

Now, what we are going to say next, may seem like contradiction but in reality, it is not.

Having not enough children can also be devastating for a nation. Extremely low birth rate poses its own dangers.

Dearth of young ones mean not enough labor force for the future. Industrialized nations will end up importing labor from other non-developed countries, which creates its own problems like language, culture, religion and other assimilation issues.

There usually will be a huge aging problem also. More aged people mean more health-related ailments. This will force governments to spend more of their scarce resources on health care expenses rather than other developments. Fewer younger people will have to sustain a large aging population. This may not sit well with the younger generation.

Another sensitive issue may be gender imbalance. In many, if not most, under-developed countries there is a traditional preference for boys as girls are considered more expensive to raise than boys. When girls get married, many parents have to accumulate enough wealth for a suitable dowry whereas boys can find better paying jobs and provide for their families. Parents hope that the boys will take care of them when they get old. So, in many countries girls are aborted or abandoned or otherwise neglected. As a result, there may be many more young men than women. Men may not be able to find suitable wives which may cause emotional as well as mental problems.

That is why in many under-developed countries, gender of a baby is not allowed to be disclosed before a birth. This makes a lot of sense.

The point is that birth rate of a nation should be able offset the death rate. It behooves each country to strike a balance between too high a birth rate and too low a birth rate. This may seem a difficult issue to resolve.

IsoloMetrik Society encourages its citizens to have minimum of two children and it limits them to a maximum of three children. Society sees no dichotomy here. If a couple wants more children, adoption is a very good option and is encouraged.

This brings up issues like second marriage, third marriage and so on. Every new couple might want a child of their own regardless of children from previous unions. We understand the sentiment. Towards that end, we recommend that a new couple might be allowed one child of their own even if they had children through prior marriages, provided they have sufficient wherewithal.

Another thorny issue is what if on rare occasions a couple gives birth to quadruplets or sextuplets?

Most logical answer is to leave it alone as long as babies are well babies.

Article 26

Society and Euthanasia

IsoloMetrik Society believes euthanasia should be legal.

In IMS, euthanasia is not only legal, but it is quite common.

A person who is terminally ill, who feels their life is not worth living due to intolerable pain or loss of basic motor functions or lack of dignity, and wants to end his/her life, they should be allowed to do so. If they need any assistance in committing suicide, full assistance must be provided. IMS believes death should be a matter of choice as long as that choice is or was made with a lucid mind. Nobody should be forced to suffer through unmitigated pain until their bodies simply give up.

Quality of life is much more important than longevity of life. But Society goes much further than this.

If a person lies in vegetative state and family promises to take care of that person, financially and in every other way, Society will respect their wishes. No public funds can be spent on a vegetative person. If family is not willing to or cannot look after that person, euthanasia will be in order. What good does it do the nation by keeping such a person alive through a myriad of tubes? Even if palliative care is available, medical funding can be better spent on infant care, child care and other social programs as well as research and innovations.

If a child is born with severe deficiencies, life of that child will be extremely diminished. It will cause undue hardships and financial burden, which family of that child has to bear, not Society. Not that Society does not want to but to what end? What kind of life will that child have? However, if the family is willing to bear that burden and take care of that child, financially and in every other way, Society has no objection. If family cannot or is not willing, Society understands that also.

In that case euthanasia would be quite appropriate.

We cannot stress enough, that all these decisions are made out of sheer compassion for the afflicted children, persons and their families and the nation at large and for no other reasons. Society takes no pleasure in it.

As always, it is our fervent hope that our compassion will not be misconstrued.

No religion will be allowed to interfere in this matter.

Article 27

Society and Adoption

IsoloMetrik Society whole heartedly encourages adoption and renders whatever help needed to make the process as smooth as possible.

Many biological parents cannot take care of their children because of drug abuse, alcohol abuse, extreme poverty or for whatever other reason there might be. Some birth parents may be penurious, homeless people, college students etc. who have not figured out life yet and are struggling to take care of themselves. In some cases, both parents may die suddenly due to an accident with no relatives to take care of young ones left behind. Some parents may severely abuse their children such that they are deemed unfit to raise them in a safe environment.

Adoption will make a very good alternative in all these cases.

When a couple decides to adopt a child, they have to know they are going to take on the responsibility of taking care of someone else's child. This is a lifelong commitment. That is why both, birth parents and potential adoptive parents, will have to go through a lengthy interview process and follow strict guidelines. IMS is fully aware that a child's most basic right is to grow up in a safe nurturing environment and has laws put in place to protect that right. Society encourages all parents, birth as well as adoptive, to ask plenty of questions, to do their own homework and research.

Society will make sure that cost of adoption process is not prohibitively high.

Illegal adoptions, black market babies are forbidden. Human trafficking in babies usually occur in densely populated and poor countries. IMS has strict laws to curb these practices. There are stringent punishments for persons caught in engaging in human trafficking. But we will address this issue in detail in later chapter.

IMS believes same sex couples have the same right to adopt a child as hetero-sexual couples. Even an individual may adopt as long as that person is well settled in life and can provide loving environment for healthy growth of the adopted child.

Adoption process may be open or closed. It may be domestic or international. It may be private (arrangement between adoptive and birth parents without involving outside agencies) or public. Each has its own advantages and disadvantages. Society does not see any need to delve into these matters here. Suffice it to say that it has structured guidelines laid out that is fair to all parties involved, keeping the child's welfare as the top goal.

Despite best efforts of all parties involved, some adoptions may and do breakdown.

We understand that. IMS is ready for such occasions. Society will be the final arbiter of any dispute. It will look for other suitable parents. If they are not available, Society will adopt them. The children then will become Society's wards; loving Society's sons and daughters.

Article 28

Society and Surrogacy

In IsoloMetrik Society, surrogacy is legal.

Society has no problem *in principle* with surrogacy. If childless couples who have some kind of medical deficiency such that they are unable to conceive on their own, Society feels surrogacy might be very helpful in making the family whole.

All participants in the process must understand or made to understand short as well as long term implications that may arise from this endeavor.

Of course, *altruistic surrogacy* would be the best option. Nothing like a womb of a close relative or a close friend, second only to one's own.

But many times, that may not be an available option. In such cases, *renting* a womb makes sense. At first glance, the word *renting* seems to have a bad connotation. But it is not, as long as there is absence of exploitation.

In many poor countries, women would be willing to carry a baby for nine months in their wombs in exchange for money. Society does not frown on it simply because this then becomes an economic activity, a business, benefiting all sides. It still sees the same benefits associated with surrogacy. It is just that the parameters have now changed.

Most of the poor, illiterate women agreeing to surrogacy may not have any concept of what is involved. They may not know what will happen to their bodies, what kind of risks will they be taking, what kind of bonds can develop between the baby and themselves, the emotional toll it may take upon parting with the child. All these things and much more must be made clear to the surrogate mother. It is a lot easier and safer if surrogate mother has children of her own because she would have gone through this maternity process before.

A contract should be signed between the surrogate mother and the couple wanting to have children with the benevolent IsoloMetrik Society looking over their shoulders. All expenses, including pre-natal care must be paid by the adopting couple on top of negotiated fee. There may be unforeseen or unexpected expenses incurred. That also is the responsibility of the couple. Remember! surrogate mother may be poor and cannot pay for anything. If surrogate mother dies during pregnancy, couple will pay for funeral expenses. The contract may or may not provide for surrogate mother to see the child after delivery. Although, Society feels, that surrogate mother should not be deprived of the joy of seeing the baby grow; the same baby that she just gave birth to. In fact, Society encourages all parties to keep in touch with each other long after the birth to keep surrogate mother abreast of the progress of the child.

Main goal of the entire process is that when end comes, everybody leaves happy and satisfied and that nobody feels cheated.

In case of any disagreement or dispute at any time, your benevolent Society will be the final arbiter, keeping in mind that the surrogate mother has relinquished all rights to the baby by signing the contract.

In IsoloMetrik Society, always, those raising a child are the real parents, not those who give mere birth.

Article 29

Society and Monogamy

IMS is a monogamous society. Monogamy is the law of the land.

Nobody is allowed to have more than one spouse. It is Society's strong feeling that that only can provide marital bliss and satisfaction to all individuals involved. It is also economically better suited as most individuals of average means cannot afford to satisfactorily maintain more than one spouse. Besides, in the eyes of the Society, it is just so immoral.

Monogamy promotes better understanding between spouses and produces noble love and affection between them. It contributes healthily to family peace, solidarity and happiness. A person can only please a single spouse physically, mentally and spiritually. Monogamous family is more stable and longer lasting as there is little scope for sexual jealousy. There is better social status for a monogamous spouse. No spouse is subservient to the other spouse.

Otherwise, Society believes, an individual is descending into an abyss full of conflicts and complications.

Punishment for polygamy is very severe in IsoloMetrik Society. Heavy financial fine may be levied. Each nation may device its own solution as long as polygamy is not allowed.

Innocent spouse with no inkling about other spouse's polygamy is just that - innocent.

Of course, suffocation of a spouse in a bad marriage is also not acceptable in IMS.

Therefore, divorce and remarriage is very easy in Society with equitable distribution of joint wealth between the spouses.

Society encourages marriage between a man and a woman. The so called *traditional* marriage. However, it is also a progressive Society and understands other sentiments too. Therefore, it does not scoff at alternate life styles. Lesbian, Gay, Bisexual and Transgender lifestyles are accepted by the Society and these individuals are treated with the same respect and rights as heterosexuals.

Society has neither the right nor the desire to dictate affairs of the heart. If a person falls in love or is physically attracted to somebody other than the spouse and has an affair, that is strictly between husband and wife. They may reconcile or file for divorce. Society may provide counseling if such parties think that would help. But that will be the extent of Society's involvement in these matters.

Article 30

Society and Organ Donations

In IsoloMetrik Society, after-death organ donation is mandatory.

IMS is a very kind, compassionate and giving Society. When a person is dead and gone, IMS believes his/her healthy organs should be harvested to help other living people in needs of such organs.

Cultural and social beliefs should not be allowed to interfere with these noble causes. Meddling by any religion will be forbidden. These and other compassionate ideas will be inculcated in the minds of middle and high school children as well as the general public so that supply of vital organs will far outstrip demand.

When that happens, wishes of people who object to harvesting their organs for whatever reasons, will be respected.

Article 31

Society and Blood Donation

Same logic applies to blood donation, although, this involves living human beings.

Since we are dealing with the living, nobody can force them to donate blood. However, everything short of force may be employed in this matter. Government may flood air waves with advertisement on a national scale. Charitable institutions also can play a major role. Best thing is to appeal to peoples' sense of compassion, their sense of belonging to the Society, the brotherhood of Society. Most will understand. And that is all that is needed.

In IsoloMetrik Society, we visualize the supply of blood far exceeding the demand.

We need to add a footnote here.

We are distinguishing donation of umbilical cord blood from regular blood donation. Blood from umbilical cord is something that every human being is born with but is routinely thrown away. After babies are born, cords are cut and clamped and are discarded. This cord blood has some remarkable qualities to cure stubborn and intransigent diseases like leukemia, sickle cell, non-Hodgkin's lymphoma and many other genetic disorders.

Society sees throwing away this umbilical cord blood as almost a criminal act. There is no way IMS can allow this practice when this blood can otherwise save untold number of lives. So, the cord blood must be donated to a blood bank. No religion or personal belief will be allowed to interfere in this matter. At the beginning of one baby's life there is a chance to save another existent life. Which other gesture can be more satisfying and fulfilling than that?

Article 32

Society and Dress Code

Every nation is different. Every culture is different. So, what is decent and what is indecent to wear will be naturally different for each country.

However, IMS does not allow people to walk naked on streets where everybody can see them. It does not allow women to walk top-less simply because men's and women's bodies are different.

This does not mean that we do not respect rights of nudists. Certain remote parks and beaches will be designated for them where they may disrobe and carry out the normal activities that people do in parks and beaches; walk, swim, play volleyball, whatever. Bold signage will alert everybody of these nudist areas.

Some women cover their hair out of modesty. That is perfectly acceptable. It is just that when women lock up their bodies wearing a full-face veil showing only the eyes, IMS feels that these women descend in to a world of twelfth century subservience. It is nothing but a walking prison. It gives the community an air of misogyny. It is as if the community is trying to hide its women and force them to lead an obscure life.

Men and women have equal status in every respect in IsoloMetrik Society. So, such dresses are illegal and simply not allowed.

Of course, while riding a bicycle or a scooter, citizens are free to cover their mouths and noses so as not to breath polluted air or dust when circumstances warrant it.

Public and private corporations as well as certain government agencies may impose reasonable restrictions on clothing at work. Customers may be denied service for not wearing shirts or shoes. Similarly, employees may be required to maintain certain dress decorum at work, depending on nature of their business.

Article 33

Society and Prayers

IsoloMetrik Society does not pretend to know whether prayer heals all wounds or brings peace to the souls who pray. All we know is that prayer is one of the tools of most religions and in the hearts of many human beings. If people believe prayer helps in healing sicknesses, diseases or problems that interfere with daily lives, who are we to dispute that belief? If they believe prayer can also help them achieve goals, dreams and other tasks they may want to accomplish in life, that is alright with Society too.

Without intimate knowledge, IMS does not want to delve into such heavy matters very deeply.

But prayers should be conducted in designated areas, not in open public places so as not to disturb or offend atheists and other non-praying public.

Each nation is different. Each has its own culture and norms. So, each country has to decide for itself whether praying in public schools will be appropriate or not. If they determine it is suitable and in accordance with their culture, prayers in public schools may be conducted before classes start. They should be very short. If schools are multi-religious, non-denominational services may be conducted. If there is a dominant religion in a school, it may conduct some sort of religious prayer on a strictly voluntary basis. Those students or whose parents or guardians object, should be free to stay away from praying.

Article 34

Society and Frivolous Lawsuits

Filing any lawsuit has a very high transactional cost. It is both expensive and time consuming to use a court to resolve any dispute.

Each nation has to decide what is frivolous and what is not. But common sense should dictate whether a lawsuit has legal merit or whether it is reasonable.

In IsoloMetrik Society, heavy financial burden is imposed on the plaintiffs as well as their lawyers for filing frivolous lawsuits so as to discourage filing such lawsuits again. In the most egregious of cases, financial fine can be such as to make the plaintiffs and their lawyers indigent. Most of such money collected should go to various social programs which the Society will have abundance of.

In IMS, a three or five-person panel of highly educated and trained people is set up under the Justice Department. This may be done for every state or province if a country is large enough. Any individual intending to file a lawsuit has to clear it as to its merits before this committee. A simple majority is needed to approve the filing. This should eliminate frivolous lawsuits.

Of course, Society's schools and parents will instill in their children good moral judgment and common sense so most of them will grow up to be upright citizens and words like *frivolous lawsuits* will be alien to them. That is our hope anyway.

Article 35

Society and Lawyers

Ultimate goal of IsoloMetrik Society is to become a lawyer-less Society. For-profit lawyer-less that is. We are not against advocacy. Advocacy is necessary.

Allow us to explain.

We are not debating the good and the bad and the ugly of work that lawyers perform.

We understand that great lawyers do a lot of good. They are always available and accessible to their clients. They not only know the law but understand their clients' businesses too. They personalize the relationship by recognizing unique styles, interests and needs of individuals with whom they work. They know how to communicate with their clients. They are always loyal to them and come fully prepared for any eventuality. They not only seek meaningful feedback from clients but act on it. They do not only what they say they will do but far exceed their clients' expectations.

There are a lot of unethical lawyers out there too, who give the profession a black eye. These scoundrels resort to barratry and scoff at the law. Clients' interest is the last thing on their minds. All they want to do is earn the biggest pay-out they can. It is no wonder that lawyers are held in such low esteem and that is all due to these greedy, unscrupulous master manipulators.

But we digress.

As we said earlier, we have no desire to discuss the good and the bad and the ugly. All we are saying is that as a kind, compassionate and loving Society, let us be your arbiter. We are not chasing commissions, we are not chasing pay-outs, we have no axe to grind. Our highly educated and trained judges don't earn any extra pay to hear your cases. You don't need to speak legalese. You don't need any fanciful words. Just simply stating your case in plain language is all that is required. Assistance of salaried advocates by the plaintiffs may be helpful and is encouraged. Judgment will not be months or years away because we know that justice delayed is justice denied. After very careful deliberations, denouement will be swift and fair.

This is what we mean by lawyer-less Society.

Article 36

Society and Parenthood

Parenting is one of the most difficult and challenging responsibilities any person can face. Society fully understands this.

Parenting styles are collections of parental attitudes and practices. Because individuals learn from many different sources including their own parents, role models, culture of the countries they live in, their own life experiences, parenting techniques can vary greatly from household to household. Society does not have any hard and fast guidelines on raising children.

Parenting is somewhat akin to teaching. It calls upon parents to assist their offsprings in the process of growing up, doing so by observing carefully the steps the children themselves take in the process and doing what is necessary to facilitate their progress. The style of the parenting with which children are raised can profoundly affect their social and psychological development, as well as their abilities to deal with life situations as adults. We understand that no one parenting style is perfectly right or completely wrong. There are no rules and regulations that are etched in stone. Neither are there any written commands or instructions. What works with one child may not work with another, even in the same household. Rigidity in parenting style is never advisable. It is a continuous lifelong job of trials and errors. It evolves with emerging situations and changing circumstances. The results are rarely hundred percent.

Most of these parenting ways are alright with IMS.

The only one that is frowned upon, is neglectful parenting. Giving a few light-handed thumps on the buttocks of misbehaving children is fine. Whipping them with a belt is a no-no and is considered irresponsible parenting. If this kind of cruel behavior becomes repeatedly egregious, putting children's normal growth patterns at risk, Society has no qualms about punishing such parents heavily. Extreme neglect or cruelty will result in extreme punishment.

IMS knows that children are its future. So utmost attention is paid to their welfare. Society aims to provide all kinds of charitable institutions to aid parents, should they need any help. And parents are encouraged to seek their help.

In IsoloMetrik Society, those who have raised a child are considered legal parents. They may or may not necessarily be biological parents.

Just like heterosexual couples, same sex couples also have the same right to parenthood. Even a single person can provide a stable, healthy environment for a child to grow up in, provided that that single person is educated and well settled in life.

In case of divorce, equal visitation rights will be invoked, depending on each situation. Child support payments will be levied on a better earning parent, until the child grows into adulthood.

Raising a child should be, for the most part, a joyous adventure. IMS strongly recommends all parents to live fully in those moments. *Don't be in a hurry*. Savor those moments. Because, once gone, they will never come back.

Article 37

Society and Bullying

IsoloMetrik Society defines bullying as intimidation of others to do what one wants through unwanted, aggressive behavior.

Everybody knows it is wrong and yet it has become a major problem in the world, especially amongst students and teenagers. Violence shown on television and movie screens, families living in poverty, uncaring parents and/or elder siblings, lack of education; they all play a part in giving rise to bullying.

Bullying can take various forms. Verbal bullying mainly involves name calling by peers. Teasing, taunting, inappropriate sexual commenting and generally embarrassing others in public places are all various forms of verbal bullying. Ills of bullying are many. It can change or ruin a person's life. The bullied can be mentally scarred for life. They may become self-conscious, shy, unsure of themselves. They become sad or depressed. They stop trusting people, denying them a chance to experience a quality relationship later in life. They may become submissive partners or may want to be left completely alone. They often develop eating disorders, begin to injure themselves. When that happens, they require extensive counseling. Bullying can leave them without a supportive group of friends they can lean on and spend time with.

Physical bullying is the oldest type of bullying. It involves hitting, kicking, punching, pushing, shoving among other things. It normally comes from one big person or kid physically harming a much smaller person or kid. The victim in such cases is often defenseless, enduring injuries that could possibly have long term or even permanent effects. In an attempt to gain power and get their self-esteem back, the bullied often become bullies themselves, thus perpetuating a vicious cycle.

Cyber bullying is something new on the world stage. It also comes in several different forms. Sending vulgar pictures of oneself on the Internet, disseminating unflattering photos to a wider group, spreading hateful messages on the web, exchanging rude comments about someone, trolling; they all fall within the sphere of cyber bullying. There are many instances of teens committing suicides due to cyber bullying as the pain and isolation becomes unbearable and they feel there is nowhere to hide.

IsoloMetrik Society is well cognizant of this problem of bullying. There is no single reason for engaging in this type of behavior as reasons are manifold. But the problem does exist and IMS is determined to prevent it. The answer lies in education. Middle and high school kids as well as teenagers will be drilled about the harmful effects of bullying. Assistance of parents and school staff will be actively sought.

Bullies resort to bullying because they feel they can get away with it. Well! bullies in IsoloMetrik Society will know that they cannot get away with bullying. Society has strict rules against bullying and those rules will be enforced. The punishment for defying these rules can be extremely severe depending on the callousness of crime.

Article 38

Society and FGM

In many countries of the world, female genital mutilation is a common practice. Girls as young as five are cut to remove their labia and that too without proper anesthetics. This is a very painful process that not only leaves physical scars but more horrifically, psychological and emotional scars that may last a life time.

IsoloMetrik Society fully understands that this practice has been going on for hundreds or even thousands of years, handed down from one generation to the next. That does not make it any less hideous. Our blood boils just thinking about it. Society is dead set against allowing such barbaric custom to flourish on its soil.

This mostly happens openly in underdeveloped, poor countries but many rich western countries are not totally immune from it. It is practiced surreptitiously, especially among migrant communities. The cutters often come for a very short period of time, cut a lot of girls and go back to their homelands right away. So, they are difficult to catch and prosecute.

Education is the key to drastically reduce or eliminate this practice. NGO's may be better suited to help curtail this practice than the government. Society encourages grass-roots organizations to create tools to assist health care workers and other professionals to detect and to take preventive steps.

For girls who are cut, IMS offers gynecology, psychology and holistic treatments that might heal their wounds.

Society has very strong judicial response to discourage such wanton violence towards its girls. Cutters and willing parents will be severely punished. Of course, each nation has to decide what the maximum punishment should be, depending on the prevailing culture.

Article 39

Society and Honor Killings

This is another one of those abhorrent crimes, usually against women, which Society finds intolerable. This one too boils our blood.

Practice of honor killing is usually found in poor, undeveloped countries. It is defined as murdering a member of one's own family for bringing shame to the family. Overwhelmingly, it is women who are the victims of this heinous act. In rare cases, men may become victims also. Fundamental difference is that males accused of dishonoring a family are usually afforded the opportunity to explain circumstances surrounding their situations and can escape death penalty by giving compensation to those who may have been dishonored. Women are rarely afforded such opportunities to tell their side of the story.

Family may be shamed if a woman chooses her own marriage partner against the wishes of her father. Women are considered personal property of men. They are a commodity owned and controlled by their fathers, husbands, brothers. Women are not supposed to express desires and feelings of their own if contrary to the wishes of fathers, husbands and brothers. Fathers usually choose grooms for their daughters and any defiance against this process is taboo.

Shame may be brought to the family if women seek divorce from their abusive husbands. They can bring shame even when they themselves are victims of rape.

IsoloMetrik Society understands that this custom has been practiced in these countries for hundreds or even thousands of years. Men in those nations may not see it as an abominable crime. So, it is difficult to mete out extremely harsh punishment to guilty parties. The key to eliminate this evil is education and persuasion. But we realize that it is a slow, tedious process.

Frankly, NGOs might be better suited for some of these tasks than governments themselves. But these human rights activists should be given adequate protection against threats and other types of harassment.

IMS cannot police the entire world. However, what it can do is to make sure honor killings do not occur on its soil.

This crime may occur in rich and developed countries also, especially amongst their migrant communities. Society has comprehensive education programs and awareness campaigns for them. It has a gamut of legal avenues and resources available for frightened victims. Needed financial assistance is also available.

Finally, for perpetrators of crime of honor killings, whether actually carried out or just planned, stringent punishment is imposed. Each country has the right to decide the maximum punishment, again based on the prevalent culture.

Article 40

Society and Acid attacks

This is a bestial act that is perpetrated by humans (mostly by men) on other human beings (mostly on women).

IsoloMetrik Society believes that throwing acid on a woman is by far the cruelest form of abusing a person which results in physical, sexual and mental suffering. It leaves the assaulted person kind of paralyzed and psychologically unable to face society confidently again. It causes severe pain, permanent disfigurement, subsequent infections, blindness and sometimes excruciating death.

This may be done for several reasons, including revenge for refusal of marriage proposal, thwarting romantic or sexual advances, perceived dishonor, land disputes, jealousy etc. Whatever the reasons, these attacks are the epitome of existing circle of violence. Mostly these dastardly acts occur in poor, under-developed, over-populated countries. Imbecile central leadership, weak or non-existent judicial system, weak or no support from police officers are the main culprits in allowing this brutal practice to continue and flourish. In many of these countries, women live under the standards of fixed marriages and dowries. When such women are brutally attacked, the government and the legal systems just look the other way and pretend as if nothing has happened. Victims are often treated as social pariah, as outcast. Sometimes they are blamed for the attacks as if it were their fault that somehow, they did something to invite these attacks.

IMS is determined not to allow such vulgar violence on its soil. One thing the Society has thoroughly grasped is that to deter any crime, punishment has to be so severe that perpetrator will not dare to commit such a crime. He knows that he cannot escape the clutches of justice in IsoloMetrik Society. He will be caught and brought to justice.

So, Society metes out punishment that will fit the crime.

IMS takes a proactive approach to mitigate these instances and has enacted strict laws to control sale, use, storage as well as international trade of acids.

Society provides very good rehabilitation services to the victims as they are crucial for sufferers to rebuild their lives. After attacks, victims face physical challenges requiring long-term surgical treatments. There are psychological challenges which demand in-depth counseling from psychologists. All these services are provided free of charge. Victims, in addition to treatments, need a shoulder to cry on, a shoulder to lean on. If victims' families do not or cannot offer that support, Society will gladly offer its shoulder.

IMS will have all kinds of institutions to aid the victims. It will provide necessary job training and find them suitable work so victims can lead useful, dignified lives.

As we have stated before, the key to eliminate this vicious crime along with all other abominable crimes is public awareness campaigns as well as educated citizenry.

And, of course, suitably harsh response from the authorities.

Article 41

Society and Human Trafficking

IMS considers human trafficking a very troubling crime and a grave violation of human rights.

Society defines human trafficking as recruitment, transportation, transfer or harboring of persons, through threat or use of force or other forms of coercion for the purpose of exploitation and monetary gain. Definition of exploitation includes not only forced prostitution, but also forced labor and slavery.

Every year, thousands of men, women and children fall into the hands of traffickers, in their own countries as well as abroad. All nations of the world are affected by this crime either as a country of origin or transit or final destination for victims.

For victims of trafficking, psychological scars may last a lot longer than any physical damage that may be inflicted upon them. Society provides very good rehabilitation services to the victims as they are crucial for them as well as their families to rebuild their lives. This will include in-depth counseling from psychologists and a shoulder to lean on. All these services are provided free of charge.

Society is a strong proponent of raising awareness of this crime and building as well as strengthening of nations' partnership and coordination and is determined not to allow such dastardly acts on its soil.

After all is said and done, IsoloMetrik Society believes that there is only one thing that will eliminate this scourge and that is enforcement of very stringent punishment for persons found guilty of human trafficking.

Article 42

Society and Child Pornography

Society defines child pornography as taking nude photos of children and filming them while they are being forced to engage in various sexual acts. Internet has made child pornography widely and easily available. It has become such an international business that it is no longer a situation of unawareness. Nor can it be neglected. It has captured mass media focus and political interest. Though the viewers are far away from the children as well as the makers of such films, they bear heavy responsibility for these distasteful crimes simply by creating a demand for distribution of the photographs.

This is one of the worst kinds of child abuse. It desensitizes children to sexual acts with adults giving them the impression that this is some kind of natural process. Many of them grow up scarred for life. It is not only offensive but illegal too. Society considers child pornography immoral and does its best to protect children living under its soil.

IMS understands completely that it is an uphill struggle due to increasing number of people supplying the material and equally increasing number demanding such material. Society has enacted very strict laws that prohibit use of a minor in making of pornography, transport of a child from one place to another, production and circulation of materials involving child pornography. It also bans sale, purchase and receipt of minors when such sale, purchase and receipt is used to produce child pornography.

Article 43

Society and Dowry System

Dowry System is illegal in IsoloMetrik Society.

Dowry means property and money that a bride brings to her husband's house at the time of her marriage. It is a custom that is prevalent mostly in underdeveloped countries. We do not know how and when this custom originated. But we suspect it has been practiced for hundreds, if not thousands, of years.

It is a curse to the bride and her parents who have to bear an enormous amount of cost to satisfy some unreasonable demands of bridegroom's party. And in many cases, these demands do not diminish after marriage. It becomes a lifelong demand. Husbands and in-laws of the bride are usually always ready to inflict harassment, insults and tortures; both physical and mental. As more and more pressure is put on the bride as well as her parents, their daughters reach a stage where the only option available is to commit suicide to free themselves and their parents from further humiliation. Many times, the parents commit suicide in the hope that that might reduce the pressure on their daughters. Wherever this practice is entrenched, it gnaws at that nation's vitality.

Instead of marriage being a union of love, it becomes a business where joy and happiness are in short supply.

This curse of dowry system must be eradicated from all lands. Just by declaring it illegal, is far from sufficient to eliminate the system. IMS will spare no cost to achieve this goal. Society will launch advertisements as well as campaigns against the system. Its laws against the dowry system will be strictly enforced. It will have voluntary social services organizations to encourage dowry-less marriages.

We have stressed many times before and it bears repeating here again that as with any ingrained ills, the key here is educated citizenry. Women must be able to get good education in schools. They must be encouraged to go to college to get even higher education and learn various trades so they can get high paying jobs. Their higher economic status will automatically discourage demands for dowry. This will empower them and they will not be subservient to their husbands and in-laws. They will also realize that their lives are not useless without marriage.

We accept the basic idea that giving gifts to the bride and her spouse to start a new life is a good thing. It helps a young, newly wedded couple to start their lives somewhat comfortably. It is every parent's wish to give to their daughters whatever presents they can afford to give. There is nothing unusual or abnormal about it. The key word here is affordability. The problem arises when the practice is forced and exceeds all bounds of reasonableness and decency. Then the system degenerates into an evil and cruel custom.

This, the Society will not allow.

Article 44

Society and Child Marriages

Child marriages are illegal in IsoloMetrik Society.

It is one of the greatest human rights violation in the world that one can imagine. There are many reasons why this unhealthy custom flourishes in many countries.

First and the foremost reason is poverty as this happens mostly in underdeveloped, overpopulated countries. Parents who have girls but do not earn much to give them a good life, often choose to marry them off early to alleviate the burden of raising them to adulthood.

Another reason is gender inequality. Even in this day and age, giving birth to a boy is considered a blessing and is celebrated whereas birth of a daughter is considered a curse and is mourned. Girls do not get proper amenities to lead a good life, but instead are forced into an early marriage.

Tradition and culture play an important role here. In many countries, the custom of child marriages has been practiced for hundreds, if not thousands of years. Parents blindly continue to follow this and do not even see the harms heaped on their daughters.

Due to increase in female harassment and molestation, many parents might feel insecure to have girls in their families. So, before they grow into adulthood, parents get them married off to elderly men, thinking, their daughters might be in safer hands for the rest of their lives.

And the biggest reason, of course, is lack of education. Neither the parents nor the girls have sufficient education to realize the many ills that come with this custom of child marriage. They do not understand that it perpetuates the cycle of poverty. Girls have to drop out of school. They usually become victims of domestic violence. As an innocent child, they do not know how to deal with a complicated married life. This in turn prompts her in-laws and spouse to inflict physical as well as mental torture. These girls may not even have entered adolescence stage of life and know nothing about sexual life but are forced to engage in physical relationship after marriage. They may suffer from pregnancy complications as their bodies have not developed enough and they may even die from child birth.

Solutions to this problem are complicated and long term. Almost all countries, including poor, underdeveloped and overpopulated ones, have enacted laws against child marriage. But they are hardly ever enforced, simply because they are extremely difficult to enforce.

We fully understand the dilemma but we are determined to find solutions.

In IsoloMetrik Society, minimum age for marriage for girls is 20 and for boys it is 21. Girls under 20 should not and cannot get pregnant. When we enunciate such statements, it is out of sheer compassion for our sons and daughters, for these boys and girls are just that. *Our sons and daughters.* Our enunciations are strictly for their well-being. There is no other motive. A fifteen, sixteen-year-old girl cannot have a child and thus ruin her life. It is like children having children. What future can this mother and child have? Teenage mothers have no time for other things because they have to be busy taking care of their babies. Most will have to drop out of school. Their struggle to deal with parenthood will be overwhelming. They will drown in a well of hopelessness and despair. It is very likely that they will become a burden on their families. Their children will grow up facing all kinds of social, psychological and economic handicaps.

Therefore, such pregnancies, by law, must be terminated. Society takes no pleasure in it but done it must be.

Sometimes, deep love is misunderstood or not understood at all. We sincerely hope, that will not be the case here.

Ultimate solution, of course, lies with educated citizenry. Children from middle school onwards will be taught about the ills of child marriages. Society will launch awareness campaigns among other things and pay due attention to the situation.

Actually, NGOs might be better suited to cure this ill than governments themselves. But then governments must ensure that these kind-hearted and noble volunteers not be threatened or harassed in any way.

Article 45

Society and Panhandling

Panhandling is illegal in IsoloMetrik Society. It has nothing to do with freedom of speech or freedom of behavior. As far as Society is concerned, it is a national shame.

Society defines panhandling very simply as begging for money or food. A nation where many of its citizens have to beg in order to feed themselves is a sign of a failed country.

Standing on a street corner and offering nominal services such as car wind-shill washing, helping park the cars, offering to carry groceries for the elderly in exchange for food or money is not considered panhandling because some work is, at least, performed to earn food or money. Panhandling is very common in poor and over-populated countries. But even rich, developed nations have seen an increase in such activities. Many countries look at someone who is out on a street corner, who is in tattered clothes, who is dirty and unshaven as blight. IMS does not look at a person that way.

There are many reasons for people to resort to panhandling. Some people may just choose this option to make a living. Society frowns on this option. For a vast number of people, though, this becomes an unwanted reality of life. It is mostly due to lack of other opportunities; lack of education, lack of jobs. Some may be mentally ill to work. Drugs and alcohol may reduce someone to a life of begging on the street for spare change. Thus, there are a great variety of individual situations forcing their hands.

Society understands.

Society is very sympathetic as well as empathetic. It knows that just banning panhandling does not resolve the underlying issues. It is a true saying that poor will always be with us. But just because poverty is endemic and intractable, does not mean that Society is clueless. There will always be soup kitchens, so nobody has to beg. Citizens are strongly urged not to give money directly to panhandlers as majority of that money will end up to buy drugs and alcohol. Instead, they are nudged to donate to non-profit charities. IMS, with the help of these charities, will have day and night shelters, food pantries, clothing distribution centers as well as medical clinics. It will also pick up physically able panhandlers and take them to job sites. Even if they have to dig ditches or sweep streets, it is better than begging.

IsoloMetrik Society sees it as the best way to build and uplift its citizenry.

Article 46

Society and Homelessness

We apply pretty much the same logic here with one glaring difference, of course. Homelessness is a state, not an activity. So, it cannot be banned.

Some may simply choose to be homeless for a much simpler life style. No electric bills to worry about, no mortgage payment, no rent money needed. Food, clothing and temporary shelter in case of inclement weather are usually available through various charitable organizations.

For most, though, homelessness is forced upon them for reasons enumerated under panhandling.

IsoloMetrik Society proposes to erect permanent tents at various designated places to eliminate homelessness. And then put most able-bodied people to do some kind of work to earn their keeps. We are under no illusion that it will be an easy task. In fact, we know it will be very difficult, at least in extremely poor, over-populated countries. They might even have to put this goal on the back burner. First food, then shelter.

Though, costs will be different for different countries, it is nevertheless doable for relatively wealthy countries. Money should be available due to very low crime rate, proper amount of taxation and good governance.

Article 47

Society and Wilderness

IsoloMetrik Society strongly believes that there is joy in walking the trail-less lush green woods and there is rapture hidden in the valleys of the mountains and the sounds of babbling brooks.

In other words, it believes in wilderness. All nations, even the poorest and most densely populated ones, must conserve and protect some kind of wilderness. It is god's creation and should not be tempered with. It is perfect the way it was created and humans should not try to meddle in it to improve it. Wilderness is an area of earth where god's creatures flourish untrammeled by humans and where man himself is a visitor.

Wilderness is a place of restraint. Wilderness is relationship. All cultures throughout history have reserved places which are different from routine and common behavior of daily life. The purpose of these special places is to reorient our focus and perceptions in a setting that is conducive to reflection. We approach such places with reverence, much more than we do the usual places in our daily lives. This kind of interaction enables us to experience unique values that wilderness provides and in turn, nurtures the human spirit. It fuels our souls and brings into focus all of the intangible goodness of life.

Wilderness is not just a geographic location, it is an *idea,* it is a *concept.* It is the way we interact with wilderness that makes it different from other landscapes. In wilderness, we are essentially preserving an endangered experience, an endangered idea that self-willed landscape has unique values and should exist. It provides sanctuary for the human spirit, where we can discover the wonder and humility so often lacking in our frenzied life. It offers an opportunity to experience a relationship between humans and nature that is becoming exceedingly rare in our hurried and harried existence. It is a relationship in which humans do not dominate but instead immerse themselves as a member of a larger community of life.

Wilderness areas allow ecological forces like forest regeneration and natural phenomena like fire to continue unabated without being manipulated by humans. It allows evolution itself to continue undisturbed.

Wilderness solitude is a state of mind, a mental freedom that emerges from settings where visitors experience nature essentially free of reminders of society. Wilderness character is much more than its physical features. It has tangible and intangible qualities. Tangible components include thriving wildlife at naturally occurring population levels. Intangible components include outstanding opportunities for adventure, discovery, mystery; places where safety and self-reliance are a personal responsibility; places which provide respite from modern civilization, its technologies, conventions and contrivances.

IMS identifies recreational, scenic, scientific, educational, conservation, historical uses as allowable public purposes. But it strongly feels that if any of these activities diminish or degrade or in any way become harmful in preserving an area's wilderness character, it should not hesitate to shut them down. Preserving the beauty of wilderness is Society's number one goal.

The unique values of wilderness will be available to Society's present as well as future generations because IMS will do everything in its power to treat wilderness as special places set apart from the conveniences and routines of modern daily life. In this endeavor, it encourages actions of every citizen, even those who may never visit but yet find their spirits nurtured just in knowing that authentic wilderness still exists in their midst.

Article 48

Society and Global Warming

IsoloMetrik Society firmly believes that global warming is real and is one of the greatest challenges facing our planet.

Rise in earth's surface temperature as a consequence of greenhouse effect is global warming. Thickening of earth atmosphere because of presence of increased carbon dioxide, nitrous oxide, methane, chlorofluorocarbon etc. is known as greenhouse effect. These greenhouse gases and other pollutants absorb more heat from the sun than they radiate back. This, in turn, causes an increase in the intensity of heat in the atmosphere. Explosive population growth, increased industrial expansion, technological advances, growing urbanization, unmitigated deforestation are some of the causes of warming of earth.

If global warming continues at current pace, existence of our world would be in danger. Global warming causes climate change with the entire globe becoming warmer and warmer. Another catastrophic consequence is the rise in sea level due to thermal expansion and arctic ice sheets melting. As a result, coastal cities and ports may be submerged under sea-water and many islands may vanish from the world map. Availability of drinking water may be even more serious crisis. Human health may be at risk as rising temperature may spread tropical air-borne and water-borne diseases more widely. The imbalance that we have created between our life and earth has already resulted in frequent disasters in the form of floods, cyclones, landslides and tsunamis. Low rainfall and rising temperature could add to the intensity and frequency of dust storms. Expanse of desert would increase. This in turn will immensely affect the quality of agricultural land, ultimately causing adverse effect on agricultural production. Droughts would be so frequent that malnutrition as well as starvation will pose serious challenge. There will be great threat to flora and fauna of the earth. Many species will become extinct. It would have far-reaching socio-economic impact.

Environmental pollution - from filthy air to contaminated water - is killing more people every year than all wars and violence in the world. Much more than smoking, hunger or natural disasters. A lot more than AIDS, T.B. and malaria combined. Financial cost from pollution related death, sickness and absenteeism is also flabbergasting. So, it is a massive problem but has yet to attract the attention it deserves from public as well as most governments.

The challenge of global warming cannot be solved by one or two nations. All countries need to come up with a comprehensive plan and then stick to it. IsoloMetrik Society strongly believes in public awareness campaigns as they can be of tremendous value. Only the masses can exert enough pressure on their governments to make them accountable.

Article 49

Society and Exotic Animal Trade

We are lumping exotic animal trade with wildlife trade here, treating them as one and the same.

The world is dealing with an unprecedented spike in illegal wildlife trade. It has become big business running into hundreds of millions of dollars. It is run by dangerous international networks much the same way as illegal drugs and arms. Poaching is a huge problem in many developing countries with abundant wild life. Elephants are killed for their ivories, rhinoceroses for medicinal value while tigers and minks are massacred for their exotic skins.

Society knows it and understands this. Not all wildlife trade is illegal, of course, but it escalates into a crisis when it becomes unsustainable, directly threatening the very survival of the species. Stamping out wildlife crime is a priority for the Society because it is the largest threat for these exotic animals, second only to the destruction of their natural habitat.

The overexploitation of wildlife should concern everybody because it affects human livelihood. Wildlife is essential to the lives of many of the world's population, often some of the poorest. They depend on local wild animals for their meat protein. They depend on their trees and plants for fuel as well as traditional medicines. Illegal wildlife trade also harms balance of nature. As human life depends on the existence of a functioning planet earth, careful and thoughtful use of wildlife species and their habitats is required to avoid not only their extinction but serious disturbances to a complex web of life promulgated by nature.

Illegal wildlife trade can also cause indirect harm through inadvertent introduction of invasive species which then prey on or compete with native species. It can cause or spread deadly diseases among pets and humans too.

IsoloMetrik Society whole heartedly supports the Convention on International Trade in Endangered Species of Wild Fauna and Flora. It is all for tightening and forcefully enforcing the ban on illegal trading. It renders help in developing programs, creating additional regulations, training enforcement personnel and funding anti-poaching organizations.

Of course, the one and the most powerful tool to address illegal and unsustainable wildlife trade is public education. Society leaves no stone un-turned to persuade consumers to make informed choices when buying wildlife-based products.

Society wants to leave these exotic and exciting wildlife to be enjoyed by its children and grandchildren.

Article 50

Society and Cyber Warfare

Cyber warfare is here and it will remain here for the foreseeable future.

We may only be a few keystrokes away from a dystopian world of no lights, no running water, no means of communications.

As far as IMS is concerned, cyber-crime may be divided into three major areas; cyber fraud, cyber vandalism and cyber terrorism. The first two are important and we have no intention of downgrading the harms caused by them.

But what keeps us awake at night is the threat of cyber terrorism. We define it as any premeditated, politically and/or financially motivated attack against information, computer systems, programs and data of a nation by terrorist groups. It is designed with only one purpose in mind; to induce total financial collapse of the enemy country. The targets may include banking facilities, military bases, power plants, air traffic control centers and water systems. A cyber-attack has the potential to create catastrophic economic damage that is so out of proportion to the low, low cost of initiating the attack. It targets extremely vulnerable computer systems, forcing them to malfunction, so that businesses, financial institutions, medical facilities and government agencies are rendered powerless.

While cataclysmic cyber-attacks are always possible, it is the mundane attacks that are likelier to cripple most countries. It is comparable to death, not by beheading but by a thousand cuts.

In the very near future, cyber warfare will be at the front and center of any conflict in addition to the well-established spheres of land, air and sea. Any nation can wage cyber war on any other nation, irrespective of resources, because most, if not all, military forces are network centric, connected to the Internet. In years to come, cyber-attack techniques are sure to be evolved even further, exposing various critical vulnerabilities that have not yet been identified.

Thus, almost all countries are plagued with crime that is easy to launch, difficult to combat, constantly changing and worst of all; border-less.

IsoloMetrik Society is determined to fight this war, tooth and nail. A very effective weapon against cyber warfare attacks is closely guarding and securing information networks. They should be updated frequently. Society will have comprehensive disaster recovery planning which will include provisions for extended outages. It will create a unified front of individual citizens, corporations and government agencies to combat this epidemic. We understand that no single group can be responsible for protection of information, trade secrets, intellectual property as well as national secrets. The security of a country depends on everyone's ability to foresee, deter and react to cyber security incidents. IMS will try and create a standard set of cyber security controls, establish laws, set penalties, in cooperation with other like-minded foreign countries.

We will also take the fight directly to the hackers. We will arrest them and severely punish them. We will name and shame foreign governments who enable cyber-attacks or host these hackers on their soil. We will not hesitate to blacklist these countries and impose crippling sanctions on them.

We understand that IsoloMetricians want the freedom and empowerment to use the technology, while at the same time to be protected against malicious attacks. And that is a huge burden which the Society gladly accepts. But we also want the citizens to know that the first step in protection starts with their awareness and knowledge.

Article 51

Society and Despicable Despots

We are sure decent people all over the world must often be wondering how one cruel dictator can, in a short period of time, destroy a thriving nation. And if they are not wondering, they should.

Unfortunately, the world is full of such barbarians.

Their crimes include enslavement, forced conscription of child soldiers, imprisonment, repression, disappearances, torture, rape and murder. In short, they are crimes against humanity. They rule by fear. Their countries are run by his crony thugs and corrupt military men. It is a horrific reign of terror and oppression, an all-pervading invisible power of evil. It is a hideous display of savagery, moral depravity, malignant vitriol. There are many examples of devastation of rich and lush lands laid waste in a span of just few years by such heartless monsters.

And who suffers the most? It is ordinary, anonymous citizens - farmers, students, housewives, young females, office workers, intelligentsia, shopkeepers. They are targeted because they are weak, unprotected, easy prey. In some cases, well known, prominent men and women get caught up and killed just to terrorize the living and subjugate the populace. To say that life is hard under such regimes would be a ridiculous understatement.

Knowing what we know about the human species, IMS does not wonder. IMS knows. IMS understands.

If there is a silver lining, if it can be called that, it is that most of these brutal regimes are tiny, puny, imbecile for the outside world at large. Thus, they are *invadable.*

Not only they are invadable; they must be invaded.

Preferably, it should be launched under the aegis of United Nations or some such world institution. Alas, experience tells us that response from so called world institutions will be pusillanimous. It is the very nature and make up of these institutions that make timid the norm. There are hundreds of countries involved with each nation having its own ulterior motive and pulling in different directions. Human suffering takes a back seat.

IsoloMetrik Society prefers a rich, powerful neighboring nation to either go it alone or launch an invasion with the support of a few other like-minded comrades-in-arms countries.

The invaded country will be a democratic nation governed by freely elected officials. It will not be allowed to have a military or army. Peace and stability will be maintained by law enforcement officials. Initially, observers from a world institution will oversee the transition until the freed nation weans itself and is able to carry on its affairs by itself.

Society wants to make it very clear that it has no selfish ends to serve. Invasion will be very temporary and quick. It is not an occupation. There are no lofty imperialistic goals. It is not a conquest. We are not seeking dominion. We are not after power or territory.

All we want to do is to free the humanity from the savage yolk of bondage, from enslavement, from repression, from torture so that ordinary folks may live in peace, freedom and liberty.

That is it.

Article 52

Society and Immigration

Every country has the right to control its borders. IsoloMetrik Society is a firm believer of this philosophy. It realizes that open border policy is suicidal not only for its resources but for its unique culture as well as character also. This has absolutely nothing to do with xenophobia.

IMS controls its borders by *any means necessary*.

This does not mean that Society does not welcome immigrants. It does. But on its own terms. It welcomes highly educated and skilled immigrants *without* a quota system, provided they enter the country legally in an orderly fashion determined by each nation. Eventually they may be allowed to obtain citizenship if they so desire. History has shown that this has helped the economy tremendously over a long haul and had little lasting impact on the wages or employment levels of native-born citizens. Skilled immigration enlarges the economy and leads to more innovation, entrepreneurship and technological prowess. Prospects for long term economic growth of most nations would be considerably dimmed without contributions of highly skilled immigrants. Family reunification, family ties take a very back seat to skills, education and an ability to assimilate.

Unskilled and uneducated immigrants are allowed in the country only if a nation needs their physical labor. They will be given work visa but will not be allowed to become permanent citizens. Once their labor is not required, they will have to go back to their native land. While living under the Society's reign, they will be treated with dignity and extreme courtesy as well as paid quite well, much more than they would earn in their own countries.

IMS does not offer automatic birth-right of citizenship to any child of an immigrant. Gaining of citizenship is quite difficult and has to be earned through education and skills. In fact, if a country wishes to remain homogenous, it is perfectly alright to offer only the work visa but not to offer citizenship to even the skilled immigrants. Nations will still draw them to their shores due to high wages and dignified treatment. Each country is free to decide whether it wants to become heterogenous or remain homogenous.

Society is very compassionate towards *persecuted* refugees pouring over its borders. It treats them humanely, by providing temporary food, clothing and shelter for a very short period of time. Every province or state will have a parcel of land earmarked for refugees. They will not be allowed outside of that area and will not be permitted to work. As soon as circumstances are right, they will have to go back to the countries they came from, even if it takes years. If possible, they will be transported to the Refugee Nation. This applies very aptly to all asylum seekers also. Our hearts go out to them and with a heavy heart we steer them to the Refugee Nation where no one will kick them in the stomach or rape them or pillage them or mutilate them. (More on the Refugee Nation later).

Society is very harsh with ruthless human smugglers plundering and otherwise taking unconscionable advantages of helpless refugees. It actively looks for them to eliminate refugee smuggling.

IMS does not recognize *economic* refugees.

In closing, we cannot help but offer this piece of advice to every country:

A nation that fails to control its borders is asking for profound economic, social and political upheaval, not to mention increased risk of terrorism.

Article 53

Society and Terrorism

Terrorism is an international problem in today's global community. Each nation has to define for itself what can be considered terrorism. For, it is true that one nation's terrorist may be another nation's freedom fighter. It is very difficult to find a proper, well-accepted definition of terrorism. Differing backgrounds and cultures along with differing histories of people are some of the many challenges in defining terrorism.

As far as IMS is concerned, use or threat of use of violence and intimidation of ordinary citizenry in the pursuit of political or financial goals is terrorism. This involves treating human lives as a means to an end.

It also fully understands that strife, injustice, oppression, torture of individuals on this earth spawns the scourge of terrorism. But Society considers this altogether another issue.

Society understands the costs of terrorism. Peace, happiness, tranquility are the ultimate victims of terrorism along with enormous financial burdens associated with it.

Society is dead set against allowing terrorism to flourish on its soil. It knows that no government can keep its legitimacy if it fails to protect its people. If Society can police the whole world, it will not allow terrorism to exist in the entire world. But it knows its limitations. It cannot police the globe.

One of the goals of terrorism is to make the terrorist's views heard. Today's terrorist is savvy about the world of media. After committing a terrorist attack, they may go on a media blitz as it is an excellent window to shout their demands and views from.

IMS has very strict policy concerning terrorism. It does not negotiate with terrorists nor does it give in to their demands. On its soil, it has some of the strongest preventive measures to mitigate acts of terrorism. Society believes in stopping the act before it occurs. Therefore, it has adopted a wide network of monitoring and surveillance systems. Any person, any residence, any institution may be monitored. This is not considered harassment in the eyes of the Society. It is thought off as wise and prudent policy. If some members of the Society feel they are being watched more intensely or more often than others, that is perfectly fine. Good of the Society comes before the good of an individual or an institution.

Society calls a spade, a spade. *Political correctness* is frowned upon.

It believes that *Intolerance of intolerance is no intolerance at all.*

Permit us to elaborate.

If we exhibit unequivocal tolerance towards unequivocally intolerant individuals, then we as a tolerant society, will not be able to withstand the torrent of intolerance spewed by these intolerants. The sad result will be the death of a tolerant, democratic nation and the demise of tolerance itself.

So, zero tolerance of intolerance makes IMS savvy and smart.

Mandatory death sentence is imposed on the terrorists. Planning an act of terrorism is as culpable as committing the act itself. Terrorists cannot get away on a technicality. Nor is insanity defense allowed. Right to privacy is discarded and unlawful searches are accepted if incriminating evidence is unearthed. If no evidence is found, Society will owe a sincere apology to the offended individual. And may be some compensation, depending on the severity of violation.

It is an art to ferret out potential terrorists. A school will be established to train highly educated and smart citizens in this art. A three (or five) persons panel of these highly trained, educated people is set up to determine guilt or innocence of terrorists. After all or most of the evidence is in, it should not take more than a week to judge guilt or innocence. If guilty, terrorist or terrorists and their abettors are usually put away within three days after extracting whatever information that needs to be extracted from these people. Terrorists will be cremated regardless of their beliefs and their ashes will not be returned to their families.

This does not mean Society has no respect for the privacy of its citizenry. It surely does. But it also believes privacy should take somewhat of a back seat to mayhem and mass casualties. The key here is a well-placed suspicion.

IsoloMetrik Society will never execute an innocent person. Burden of proof of guilt is Society's and the accused is innocent until proven otherwise. Some sort of video or verifiable audio or DNA evidence would suffice.

Article 54

Society and Refugee Nation

Often, we have wondered how humans can inflict so much pain on so many other human beings and we have witnessed with equal amazement the human capacity to tolerate such suffering and despair. It is almost lyrical, but for the sadness of it.

On second thoughts, we do not wonder. We know and we understand humans. The evil that they are capable of inflicting on their own kind.

In the midst of this indescribable, untold miseries, we propose to create a Refugee Nation in a vast land somewhere in this world, under the aegis of United Nations or similar such institution.

Anybody who wants to flee their native countries due to genuine fear of their own or their families' safety, may come to this Refugee Nation created for just this reason. Economic reasons cannot be part of the criteria.

Rich nations should assist in helping settle these people. In fact, it is in their best interest to do so as they can control their borders better. Hopefully, for many refugees, it will be their temporary residence, until they can safely go back to their own motherland. Although, somehow, we have a sinking feeling, a sneaky suspicion, that for many refugees, this will become their permanent home. Unfortunately, we see it as one of the largest, most densely populated nations on earth, a conurbation of tortured souls.

But at least, nobody in Refugee Nation will kick them in the stomach, rob them, rape them or otherwise pillage them. Strict surveillance will be maintained. Gangs will not be allowed to flourish. Prostitution out of desperation will not be necessary. No speck of corruption nor any other unseemly rackets will be tolerated. In fact, no illegal activity or crime can be committed. Stringent punishment will be imposed for defying the rule of law.

No religious edifices will be allowed to be erected. After all, religion is one of the root causes of conflicts in this world. This does not mean that praying is banned. No, not at all. But people will have to pray in their own tents or huts in their own minds. In fact, this is encouraged as it will help sooth frayed nerves. Refugees will not be segregated either by nationality nor by religions.

Refugee Nation will be a real nation teeming with real, live human beings. It will have schools, playgrounds, markets and hospitals along with anything else imaginable. Small legal businesses will be allowed to flourish in this nation.

Family planning will be absolutely mandatory and will be strictly enforced. Birth of no more than two children will be allowed per family. If they have at least two children before they enter refugee nation, they will not be allowed to produce any more children under any circumstances. Plenty of birth control devices will be made available.

These refugees will not be forgotten or stripped of their identity. They are victims of human cruelty but not faceless victims. Constant efforts should be made to repatriate them safely to their own homelands.

We are under no illusion that Refugee Nation will be a panacea for its denizens. For, what will unite these people, will be an inextinguishable desire and hope for a little bit better, a shade more decent life *somewhere else*. Though, we do realize, overwhelming majority of them will live and die in Refugee Nation.

If rich, industrialized countries wish to welcome some of the skilled refugees to their own land after careful vetting, such gestures will be encouraged. These nations may exclude any body they wish to exclude from consideration as this is a favor and not an obligation.

Footnote:

We believe a footnote is in order here.

What we have done on previous pages is try to enumerate and explain our thoughts and principles that may be universally applied to all countries. Naturally, each and every country is unique economically, socially, culturally and every which way one can imagine. Different norms, different beliefs, myriad of practices in daily lives make situations extremely complex. There is no silver bullet. No single solution is going to fit hundreds of nations of the world. Implementation of solutions as well as costs associated with it can never be predicted ahead of time as process will be dramatically different for each country.

Hence, the brevity of the book.

What we have to do is that when a nation decides to embrace IsoloMetrik concept, we have to thoroughly study the uniqueness of that country to help implement *IsoloMetrism* with the cooperation of that nation's honorable citizens, scholars and other wise men and women.

Epilogue I

Whenever, wherever humans are involved, there is no such thing as perfection. However, IsoloMetrik Society is as close to utopian perfection as one can ever hope to dream.

Epilogue II

It is our fervent hope that this little book will create such a revolution that sooner or later the whole world will want to become an IsoloMetrik world. People will rise up and say "Let us go IsoloMetrik and save our country". When that happens, this book will become a guiding force for them.

Author can be reached at
nikhilmodi49@gmail.com

Or on Twitter @nikhil_modi

Or at www.facebook.com/nikhil.modi.773

Made in the USA
Columbia, SC
10 September 2018